A BEGINNERS GUIDE TO MODERN ELECTRONIC COMPONENTS

D1101061

Other Titles of Interest

A BEGINNERS GUIDE TO MODERN ELECTRONIC COMPONENTS

by

R. A. PENFOLD

BERNARD BABANI (publishing) LTD
THE GRAMPIANS
SHEPHERDS BUSH ROAD
LONDON W6 7NF
ENGLAND

Please Note

Although every care has been taken with the productionof this book to ensure that any projects, designs, modifications and/or programs etc. contained herewith, operate in a correct and safe manner and also that any components specified are normally available in Great Britain, the Publishers do not accept responsibility in any way for the failure, including fault in design, of any project, design, modification or program to work correctly or to cause damage to any other equipment that it may be connected to or used in conjunction with, or in respect of any other damage or injury that may be so caused, nor do the Publishers accept responsibility in any way for the failure to obtain specified components.

Notice is also given that if equipment that is still under warranty is modified in any way or used or connected with home-built equipment then that warranty may be void.

© 1990 BERNARD BABANI (publishing) LTD

First Published — June 1990
Reprinted — February 1994

British Library Cataloguing in Publication Data
Penfold, R. A.
   A beginners guide to modern electronic components
   1. Electronic equipment. Components
   I. Title
   621.3815

ISBN 0 85934 230 1

Printed and bound in Great Britain by Cox & Wyman Ltd, Reading

Preface

There have been vast changes in electronics over the past twenty-five years or so, and not least of these is the massive increase in the number of components available. In particular, the number of semiconductors available twenty-five years ago was strictly limited, whereas there must be thousands of these components listed in the current electronic components catalogues. Even with components such as capacitors and the humble resistor, there are now many types to choose from.

The purpose of this book is to provide practical information to help the reader sort out the bewildering array of components currently on offer. An advanced knowledge of the theory of electronics is not needed, and this book is not intended to be a course in electronic theory. The main aim is to explain the differences between different components of the same basic type (e.g. carbon, carbon film, metal film, and wire-wound resistors) so that the right component for a given application can be selected. In a book of this size it is not possible to cover every single electronic component currently available. The number of specialised components currently in existence, particularly the numerous dedicated integrated circuits, is simply too great to permit this. However, a wide range of components are included, with the emphasis firmly on those components that are used a great deal in projects for the home constructor.

R. A. Penfold

Warning

Certain Components may carry mains voltages.

Never work on mains powered equipment unless it is disconnected from the supply unless you are absolutely certain that you know what you are doing.

Remember that capacitors can hold their charge for quite some time even after the supply has been disconnected.

Contents

Chapter 1

PASSIVE COMPONENTS

Passive components are amongst the most simple of electronic components, but are essential to virtually every circuit, even in these days of sophisticated integrated circuits. I suppose that any component which does not provide amplification (switching or linear) could be described as a passive component. However, it is usually taken to mean resistors, capacitors, and inductors, and this is the narrow definition we will use here. Passive components such as switches and diodes are covered in other chapters.

Resistors

Resistors are probably the most common components in the majority of circuits and, fortunately, they are just about the cheapest electronic component. There are two types of resistor circuit symbol in common use, and these are the box and zigzag types (Figure 1.1). I think that I am right in stating that the box style is the one that conforms to the British standard, but the zigzag type has been in widespread use for a great many years, and seems likely to continue in

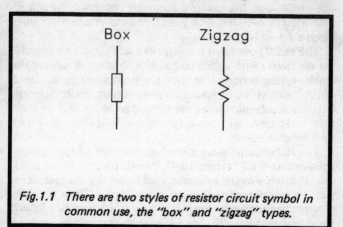

Fig.1.1 There are two styles of resistor circuit symbol in common use, the "box" and "zigzag" types.

use for some time to come. It is the resistor symbol used by a number of electronics magazines published in the U.K., and is one that you are therefore likely to encounter quite a lot.

The function of a resistor, as its name suggests, is to resist the flow of an electric current. Ohm's Law states that resistance equals voltage divided by current. Therefore, if a potential of 6 volts produces a current flow of 2 amps, the resistance through the circuit is 3 ohm (6 volts divided by 2 amps equals 3 ohms). Resistors having values from under one ohm to components having values of at least ten million ohms are available. High values are usually given in kilohms (1 kilohm or 1k = 1000 ohms) or megohms (1 megohm or 1M = 1000000 ohms).

Physical Composition

Physically, resistors are mostly cylindrical and have axial leads (i.e. a lead protruding from each end of the cylinder). Vertical mounting types are produced, but seem to be little used these days, and do not seem to be available from component retailers. The size of resistors varies from a few millimetres long for low power types, to several centimetres long in the case of higher power types. The power rating is in watts, and these days it represents something very close to the maximum power that the component can withstand continuously without overheating. At one time they were designed to be able to take a 100% overload, so a ½ watt resistor of about 30 years ago is a 1 watt resistor these days!

The exact power that a resistor can safely handle is dependent on factors such as the length of its leadout wires, and the ambient temperature. In practice it is advisable to use a resistor well within its maximum power rating, preferably with it continuously dissipating no more than about half its rated power. In general, the cooler components operate, the better their reliability.

In catalogues resistors are often described as having compositions such as "carbon film", "metal oxide", wire-wound, etc. This refers to the substance used to provide the resistance, and the wire-wound type is the most simple. These components normally take the form of a tube which acts as a former for a coil of wire. The wire used is resistance wire, and the

2

value of the component is controlled by the length of wire used (greater lengths of wire giving proportionally greater resistance) and the grade of resistance wire. The resistance wire and the connections to the leadout wires are usually covered over with a protective layer of cement or some similar material.

Wire wound resistors are mainly used where high powers must be dissipated, and they mostly have power ratings of about 3 watts to 20 watts. They are mostly designed to be able to operate quite hot, and may operate beyond 100 degrees Centigrade if taken close to their maximum power rating. Consequently, they should not be positioned close to any heat sensitive components. They are not very good for use in high frequency circuits since their coil-type construction inevitably gives them a significant inductance. This can give unpredictable results at frequencies above a few hundred kilohertz. Some wire-wound resistors have the winding in two sections which are wound in opposite directions. This minimises the inductance of the component, but in practice might not entirely eliminate the inductance problem. It is only fair to point out that other types of resistor also exhibit a certain amount of inductance, which is inevitable as even a straight piece of wire a few millimetres long has a small amount of inductance. However, with other types of fixed value resistor the inductance, provided the leadout wires are kept short, is usually insignificant.

The standard type of resistor in days gone-by was the carbon type. This type of resistor takes the general form depicted in Figure 1.2. Basically it consists of a ceramic tube which has a seal and a leadout wire at each end. The tube is filled with carbon, or to be more precise, it is filled with a mixture of carbon and a ceramic material. The latter helps to bond everything together, and as it has a very high resistance, it increases the value of the component. The value can therefore be set at approximately any desired figure (within reason) by using the appropriate mixture of carbon and ceramic material.

Although delightfully simple to make, and hence quite cheap to manufacture in large numbers, this type of resistor does have its limitations. The two main problems are noise

3

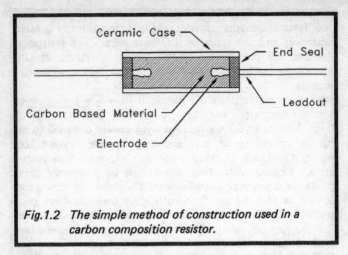

Fig.1.2 The simple method of construction used in a carbon composition resistor.

and stability. A small amount of noise is not of great importance in many applications, but it is crucial in the early stages of audio circuits, or any sensitive linear circuits in fact. In the past the level of noise produced by carbon resistors was probably insignificant in comparison to the noise generated by the active components. Advances in semiconductor technology and the widespread use of high quality digital audio systems has changed this situation, necessitating the use of higher quality passive components.

The second problem is one of stability. All resistors are prone to changes in value caused by temperature changes, but carbon types are amongst the worst in this respect. There is a secondary problem in that their values can change by a significant amount with the passage of time. Again, other types of resistor are not immune to this problem, but suffer it to a far lesser degree. Carbon composition resistors are suitable for non-critical applications, but seem to be little used at all these days.

The new standard type of resistor is the carbon film type. These have the basic make up shown in Figure 1.3. Like a carbon resistor, a ceramic former again acts as the basis of the component. An electrode and a leadout wire are fitted at each end of the component. Unlike the ordinary carbon type, the

4

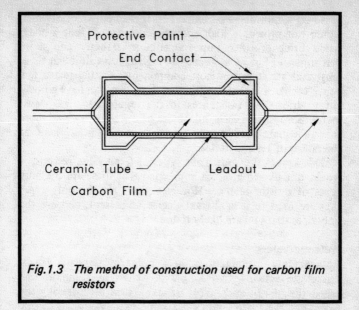

Fig.1.3 *The method of construction used for carbon film resistors*

Labels in figure: Protective Paint, End Contact, Ceramic Tube, Carbon Film, Leadout

carbon material is on the outside of the former in the form of a thin film, rather than a solid block of material inside the former. The resistance of the component is governed by the exact composition of the carbon based film, and to some extent by the thickness of the film. This second point is important, as it enables precise values to be obtained by cutting a helical groove into the film, so as to trim the value to precisely that required.

These resistors are cheap to manufacture in large numbers, can easily be made with tolerances of 5% or better, are very rugged, have much lower noise levels and temperature co-efficients than ordinary carbon types, and are affected less by ageing. It is perhaps not surprising that they are now the type of resistor that is most widely used.

Where even higher performance is required, metal film resistors are normally used. The construction of these components is very much the same as that of carbon film components. The obvious difference is that they use a metal film rather than a carbon type. To be more accurate, they are

5

based on a film of metal oxide, rather than pure metal (which would not provide a high enough resistance). Using a metal oxide brings further improvements in stability and noise performance, but at a somewhat higher cost (although these must still count as low cost components, costing just a few pence each). Like carbon film resistors, they can have grooves cut to trim their resistances to the required figures. Most metal film resistors have tolerances of 2% or better, and more than adequate stability to justify manufacturing them to tolerances of 1% and better.

This covers the four main types of fixed value resistor. I would not like to give the impression that these are the only types of resistor in use. However, these are the only types that are used to a significant degree at present, and are the only ones that you are likely to use.

Preferred Values

Resistors are manufactured in a range of standard values. There are actually two ranges of values in common use, called the "E12" and "E24" series. These are basically the same, but the "E24" series has some extra values, as can be seen from this list, which shows both series of values.

E12	E24
1.0	1.0
–	1.1
1.2	1.2
–	1.3
1.5	1.5
–	1.6
1.8	1.8
–	2.0
2.2	2.2
–	2.4
2.7	2.7
–	3.0
3.3	3.3
–	3.6
3.9	3.9
–	4.3

6

E12	E24
4.7	4.7
–	5.1
5.6	5.6
–	6.2
6.8	6.8
–	7.5
8.2	8.2
–	9.1

Although this list would tend to suggest that only values from 1 ohm to 9.1 ohms are available, the same values but in different decades are also available. For example, values such as 100 ohms, 110 ohms, 120 ohms, 130 ohms, etc. can be obtained. The highest value available from most component retailers is 10 megohms, but higher value resistors are manufactured. In the case of very high value resistors (about 100M) they are special glass bodied types which are supposed to remain untouched by human hands. Apparently, grease etc. from your fingers can get onto the body of resistors of this type, and effectively alter their resistance to a significant degree. At the other end of the range there are components having values in the sub one ohm decades, such as 0.1 ohms, 0.11 ohms, 0.12 ohms, 0.13 ohms, etc. Most electronic component retailers only supply values down to one ohm, but some retailers stock lower values, especially in the higher power ratings. However, the range of values available may be rather limited.

Colour Codes

Resistance values are normally shown on components in the form of colour codes, rather than simply having the values written on. This does make things a bit difficult for newcomers to electronics, but it does have its advantages. With experience, you learn to quickly recognise resistor codes so that you can pick out a component of the required value from an assortment of resistors on the workbench. If lettering on a component becomes partially erased, the value is likely to be rendered unreadable, or worse still, the apparent value might be totally wrong. Resistor colour code bands can be largely obliterated and still reveal the correct value with no difficulty.

The only real drawback of colour coding, apart from having to learn the codes when you take a practical interest in electronics, is that the colours are not always quite as obvious as one might wish. In particular, when viewing resistors under artificial light the colours are not always what they might seem, even if you have good colour vision. The problem mainly occurs when ordinary tungsten bulbs are used, and it normally manifests itself in the form of too much apparent redness in the colours. In other words, yellow can appear as orange, orange can appear red, and sometimes red can seem to be brown (or vice versa). This is not a major problem, but it pays to be on your guard when dealing with any colour coded components under tungsten lighting, especially if the lighting is not particularly bright.

I suppose that there is another drawback to resistor colour codes in that there are several closely related coding systems in use. Having learned one it is not difficult to deal with the others, but it can make things a little confusing at times. Here we will consider all three methods that have been used in recent years, plus components which simply have their values written onto their bodies using alpha-numeric characters.

If we start with the latter, this method is mainly only used on high power resistors these days. A lot of the current lower power resistors are so small that writing the values onto them in this way would be impractical. The values could be written on with no difficulty, but you would need a high power magnifier in order to read them! Values are normally in the form used on circuit diagrams. In other words, the letter that is used to denote the units in use is also used to indicate the decimal point. Thus a resistor of 2.7 ohms in value would have the value marked as "2R7", one of 10 kilohms in value would be marked "10k", and one of 1 megohm in value would be marked "1M" or possibly "1M0".

Resistors never have precisely their marked values, but are guaranteed to be within certain limits. These limits are given in the form of a percentage tolerance. As an example, a 1k resistor having a 5% tolerance rating would have an actual value of between 1.05k (1k plus 5%) and 0.95k (1k minus 5%).

8

If the value is written on a component, then the tolerance might also just be written on in the same way ("2%" or whatever). Incidentally, with higher power resistors the power rating is often shown as well (with smaller resistors their physical size is the only guidance as to their power ratings). The tolerance is sometimes indicated by a code letter, and this is a system that is also used with some types of capacitor. This is a list of the code letters and the tolerance values they represent.

Letter	Tolerance
F	1%
G	2%
H	2.5%
J	5%
K	10%
M	20%

The original form of resistor colour code bands, and what is still probably the most common type, is the four band system shown in Figure 1.4. The first two bands indicate the first two digits of the value. As an example, suppose that the first two colours are red and violet. From the table provided, you will

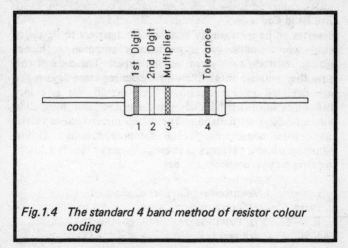

Fig.1.4   The standard 4 band method of resistor colour coding

9

see that these colours represent "2" and "7" respectively when they appear in the first two bands. The first two digits of the value are therefore 27. Note that the first band is the one nearest one end of the component.

The third band is the multiplier, and you simply multiply the first two digits by the value represented by this band. If we continue our example, and assume that the third digit is orange, as a multiplier this colour represents 1000. The value of our example resistor is therefore 27000 ohms (27 x 1000 = 27000), or 27k in other words. A method many people find easier, is to first take the value that the colour of the third band would represent if it was band one or band two. In this example, orange obviously represents 3 if it appears as band one or band two. Simply add to the first two digits the number of zeros indicated by the third band. In our example, adding three zeros to 27 again gives 27000 ohms, or 27k. Obviously this only works for resistors of ten ohms or more in value, but the vast majority of resistors are in this category.

The fourth band indicates the tolerance rating of the resistor. Continuing our example, a resistor having a gold band as the fourth one would have a tolerance rating of 5%. Our resistor having the colour code of red, violet, orange, gold would therefore be a 27k 5% type.

Five Band Codes

It seems to be increasingly common for resistors to have five band colour codes. It is particularly common on higher quality resistors, such as metal film types. The code of this type that you are most likely to encounter these days is the one depicted in Figure 1.5. This should not give any difficulties since it is basically just the original four band code plus an added fifth band. The latter merely indicates the temperature coefficient of the component, which is not normally of any practical interest. Anyway, this is a list of the temperature coefficient codes.

Colour	Temperature Co. (per degree C.)
Black	200 ppm
Brown	100 ppm
Red	50 ppm

Colour	Temperature Co. (per degree C.)
Orange	15 ppm
Yellow	25 ppm
Blue	10 ppm
Violet	5 ppm
Grey	1 ppm

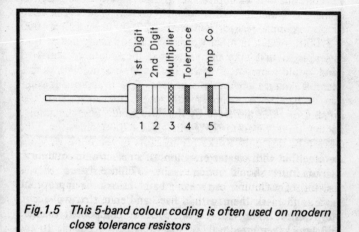

Fig.1.5 This 5-band colour coding is often used on modern close tolerance resistors

On all the resistors of this type that I have encountered the fifth band has been red, indicating a temperature coefficient of 50 parts per million per degree Centigrade.

There is another form of five band colour code, but this is one which I have not encountered much in recent times. It is another variation on the normal four band type, as can be seen from Figure 1.6. It differs from the four band type only in that three bands are used to indicate the first three digits of the value, rather than having two colours here to indicate the first two digits. Thus a colour code of orange, white, black, red, brown, gives 390 as the first three digits of the value. Red is a multiplier of 100, giving a total value of 39k (390 x 100 = 39000 ohms or 39k). Finally, the brown band indicates that the resistor has a tolerance rating of 1%.

This form of colour coding is generally only used on close tolerance resistors, and the additional band enables values to

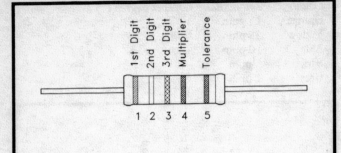

Fig.1.6 This 5-band coding is used for some close
tolerance resistors

be specified with greater precision. If an electronic equipment
manufacturer should require some 37.8k resistors, then a
resistor manufacturer can make a batch having the appropriate
value, and mark them with a five band code that will accurately reflect their value. As electronic component retailers
only stock preferred values, this is largely academic to the
amateur user. If you should encounter resistors which have
this method of coding, it is virtually certain that they will be
standard values from the E24 range, and that the third band
will be black (0).

Four Band Colour Code Details

Colour	First/Second Band	Third Band	Fourth Band
Black	0	1	—
Brown	1	10	1%
Red	2	100	2%
Orange	3	1000	—
Yellow	4	10000	—
Green	5	100000	0.5%
Blue	6	1000000	0.25%
Violet	7	10000000	0.1%
Grey	8	—	—

Colour	First/Second Band	Third Band	Fourth Band
White	9	–	–
Gold	–	0.1	5%
Silver	–	0.01	10%
None	–	–	20%

Potentiometers

Potentiometers have the circuit symbols shown in Figure 1.7(a), As will be apparent from Figure 1.7, like fixed value resistors, they have both the box and zigzag style circuit

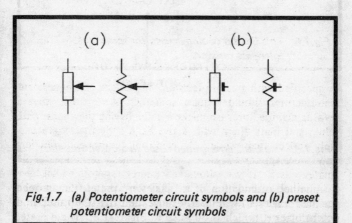

(a)   (b)

*Fig.1.7   (a) Potentiometer circuit symbols and (b) preset
            potentiometer circuit symbols*

symbols. A potentiometer has a track that is made from a carbon based material in most instances, but is often wire-wound in the case of higher power types. A terminal is connected to each end of this track, and there is a fixed resistance through the track (and therefore between these two terminals). The third terminal connects to a wiper contact that can be moved from one end of the track to the other. Most potentiometers are rotary types, having a circular track that covers 270 degrees or so. The wiper contact is then controlled via a rotating spindle. Slider types are often used in audio equipment, and these have a straight track with a wiper contact that is controlled via a sliding "spindle".

13

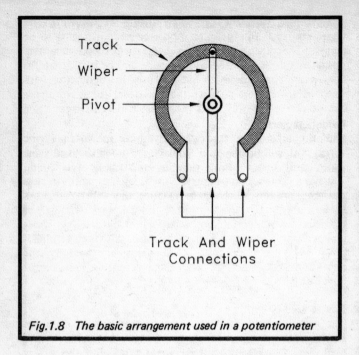

Track

Wiper

Pivot

Track And Wiper
Connections

Fig.1.8 The basic arrangement used in a potentiometer

A visual examination of a "skeleton" preset (i.e. an open construction type) will clearly show the basic setup used in a potentiometer, which is outlined in Figure 1.8. These preset potentiometers are actually somewhat more simple than the standard variety, which often have twin wiper contacts and a special lubricant, in order to increase the operating life and give lower noise levels when the component is adjusted. There are also expensive multi-turn "trimpots". The physical make up of these varies somewhat, but a common arrangement is to have what is basically a slider type potentiometer, but with the wiper contact mounted on a horizontal screw thread. As the screw is turned, the wiper contact moves along it. However, it obviously takes a number of turns to move the slider contact from one end of the track to the other. Typically it takes about ten to twenty turns for one complete traverse of the track.

Combined with the very high quality of the track and wiper contacts, this permits very precise adjustments to be made. The precision with which inexpensive preset potentiometers can be adjusted is often very limited. They are for non-critical applications, or must be used in conjunction with fixed value resistors so that the bias level (or whatever) is almost correct anyway, and the preset is only used for "fine tuning" purposes.

If a potentiometer is used as a variable resistor, only the wiper contact and one track contact are used. Adjusting the wiper contact then places more or less track between it and whichever track connection is used, giving more or less resistance in the process. In practice the wiper contact is often connected to the otherwise unused track terminal, as this can give reduced noise when the track and (or) wiper contact start to become seriously worn. All three terminals must be used when these components are used as true potentiometers, such as in volume controls and similar applications.

Log or Lin

The values of potentiometers are usually written onto the body of the component as "47k", or whatever. Colour codes are occasionally used on preset types, but this is very rare these days. The normal system of colour coding is to have coloured spots which show the value in the same way as the first three bands of the ordinary resistor colour coding. The tolerance is not normally marked, but for virtually all potentiometers is a very generous 20%! Even high quality types generally only have a tolerance of some 10%.

Potentiometers can be of two varieties: the logarithmic and linear types. They are normally marked "log" or "lin", as appropriate, next to the value marking. Note that preset types often lack this type of marking, but are only generally available as linear types. Assume preset types to be linear potentiometers unless you have reason to believe otherwise. The terms logarithmic and linear, in the present context, seem to cause a lot of confusion, as does knowing which type to use for a given application. This is all really quite straightforward though.

A linear potentiometer could reasonably be regarded as the standard type. In theory, each millimetre of track provides exactly the same amount of resistance as every other millimetre of track. Consequently, if the wiper is positioned at the middle of the track, there will be equal resistance between each track terminal and the wiper. In reality, potentiometers are mostly not made with a great deal of precision, and some pieces of track have more resistance than others. The track of a linear type has a reasonably linear characteristic though.

A common application for potentiometers is as volume controls in audio equipment. There is a problem if a linear potentiometer is used as a volume control, in that as the control is advanced, initially a small amount of adjustment gives a large increase in the volume. The next two hundred or so degrees of rotation then seem to have very little effect! This is not due to a fault in the potentiometer, but is a consequence of the way in which human hearing operates. In order to permit very quiet sounds to be heard, but loud sounds to also be heard properly, the human hearing mechanism tends to compress dynamic levels. Thus, a steady increase in volume is heard as a definite increase initially, with relatively little apparent change thereafter as the compression of the hearing mechanism comes into effect.

A logarithmic potentiometer has a non-linear track resistance that is designed to counteract this problem. It gives a relatively small increase in volume initially, with an ever larger increase as it is adjusted in a clockwise direction. This gives what, to anyone listening to the audio output, sounds like a steady increase in volume. This makes the volume much more easy to adjust accurately than when using a linear potentiometer.

Practical logarithmic potentiometers do not normally have a track resistance that provides an accurate logarithmic response. Instead, they have what is effectively a two stage track, with part of the track being made from a higher resistance material than the rest. A graph of rotation versus resistance would therefore consist of two straight lines at angles to one another, not a steadily changing curve. Although you might expect this kinked response to be obvious in use, it

16

is a reasonable approximation to the correct curve, and is not normally apparent. The obvious advantage of this method of construction is that it is relatively cheap and simple, requiring only two grades of track material.

Logarithmic potentiometers are not only used for volume controls, and they can give a better control characteristic in some other applications. However, these are relatively few and far between, and for the vast majority of non-volume control applications it is linear potentiometers that are used. For some types of circuit it is an anti-logarithmic law potentiometer that is required. Probably the best known application of this type is the Wien oscillator type audio signal generator. A linear potentiometer provides a frequency scale that gets very cramped towards its high frequency end. A logarithmic type simply exacerbates the problem, but an anti-logarithmic potentiometer gives a linear scale, or something close to it anyway.

Unfortunately, anti-log potentiometers are difficult or impossible to obtain, and compromises often have to be made. In this example, either the non-linear scaling provided by a linear potentiometer has to be accepted, or a logarithmic potentiometer connected in reverse can be used (i.e. the connections to the track terminals are swopped over). This gives a reverse reading scale, with clockwise rotation of the control knob giving decreased output frequency, but the scaling is reasonably linear. This is certainly a useful dodge to keep in mind.

Potentiometers, but not preset types, are available as dual gang components. These are effectively two components having a common spindle so they are adjusted in unison. Dual gang types are available in both the slider and rotary varieties. They are mainly used in stereo audio equipment, where one section is used in each stereo channel. However, there are other applications that require dual gang potentiometers, including the Wien oscillator type audio signal generators mentioned previously. Twin gang potentiometers are manufactured having gangs of different values, but these do not seem to be available from retail outlets. You must settle for both gangs having the same value, and will probably have a very restricted range of values to choose from.

It should perhaps be pointed out that potentiometers are in general only available in a relatively restricted range of values. The popular carbon potentiometers are mostly only available in values of 1k, 2k2, and 4k7, plus their decades up to a maximum value of 2M2. Some manufacturers produce them in values of 1k, 2k5, and 5k, plus their decades up to a maximum of 2M5. There should be no problem if (say) a 2k2 potentiometer is used where a 2k5 type is specified, or vice versa. Wire-wound potentiometers are generally larger, have higher power ratings, and are available in lower values (down to about 22R). Preset resistors are available over a somewhat wider range of values, with something like 100R to 4M7 being quite typical.

Something you should keep in mind when dealing with power ratings for potentiometers is that the specified maximum power is the highest one to which the full length of track should be subjected. If the component is being used as a variable resistance, and is set at about half resistance, only half the track will be used. Accordingly, its effective maximum power rating is halved.

In component catalogues you will often encounter "cermet" potentiometers, which are available as both standard and preset components. These are much like ordinary carbon types in essence, but the tracks are made from a glassy metal oxide material which is fired onto an alumina substrate. This gives much harder wearing tracks, permits higher power ratings to be obtained, and also permits components of closer tolerance to be produced. However, the tolerance of these components is still only 10% in most cases.

Specials

Apart from ordinary fixed resistors and potentiometers, there are a few special types that are worth including here. One of these is the thermistor, which is a temperature sensitive resistor. As already pointed out, all resistors provide a change in resistance with variations in temperature. Whereas resistors are designed to minimise this effect, thermistors are designed to produce relatively large changes in resistance from a given temperature change. All the types I have encountered have been negative temperature coefficient types. In other words, a

18

rise in temperature produces a reduction in resistance. Thermistors can be based on a number of substances, but a compound of nickel magnetite seems to be the one most commonly used.

Physically these thermistors are mostly disc shaped components about 8 to 10 millimetres in diameter, and having radial leads. Some are tubular components, rather like miniature wire-wound resistors in appearance. They can be used in temperature measuring applications, and have been used in this role quite successfully. However, they do not provide good linearity over a wide temperature range, and they are not often used in this application. Alternatives such as simple silicon diode sensors offer superior accuracy in many temperature measuring applications. A more common role for thermistors is in thermostats, where linearity is often of little importance. They are also used in temperature compensation circuits, such as bias current stabilisation in the output stages of audio power amplifiers.

Another use of thermistors is in gain stabilisation circuits in audio signal generators of the Wien oscillator type. These are capable of producing a very high quality sinewave output, but only if the level of feedback is carefully controlled so that the circuit is prevented from oscillating too violently. The type of thermistor used in this application is a special "self-heating" type. It is housed in an evacuated glass envelope that, as far as possible, insulates it from the ambient air temperature. The basic idea is that if the oscillator should oscillate too strongly, a strong current will flow through the thermistor, resulting in it getting hotter. This causes its resistance to fall, which in turn increases the amount of negative feedback so that the gain of the amplifier is reduced, and less strong oscillation results.

If loading or some other factor should result in a reduced output level, the current through the thermistor will drop, its resistance will rise, and there will be less negative feedback. This gives more gain from the amplifier, and an increased output level. It will be apparent from this that a negative feedback action stabilises the output level of the oscillator. An advantage of a thermistor in an automatic gain control circuit of this type is that it provides pure resistance, and does not introduce significant amounts of distortion. I suppose that these components could be used in other applications, and probably are. I have only ever seen them used in high quality audio signal generators though. The only common example of a self-heating thermistor is the RA53, which also seems to be sold as a type R53 thermistor.

Photo-resistors were once the most popular type of photocell, but these days they seem to have fallen from favour slightly. With their quicker response times and other potential advantages, semiconductor photo-cells seem to have largely taken over. Photo-resistors of the cadmium sulphide variety still seem to be used to a significant degree though, and are perfectly adequate for many non-critical applications.

The high sensitivity and low cost of the ever popular ORP12 photocell makes it an obvious choice for many applications. The sensitivity varies quite significantly from one type to another, and in general the larger types are more sensitive than the glass encapsulated miniature types. The latter tended to be rather expensive, and would now seem to be difficult to obtain. The ORP12 is still readily available though, and has a minimum dark resistance of 1M (often over 10M in practice), and a maximum bright resistance of no more than 80 ohms. This can be equalled or bettered by some modern semiconductor photo devices, but these are really two stage components which have a sensor and an amplifier. The sensitivity of the ORP12 and similar cadmium sulphide cells is extremely impressive for what are truly passive devices, having no form of built-in amplification. If you look at the sensitive surface of an ORP12 you can clearly see the zigzag shape of the light sensitive material. This gives a large effective surface area, which aids the high sensitivity.

A useful property of cadmium sulphide cells is that they have a spectral response which is similar to that of the human eye. However, most types (including the ORP12) cover a somewhat wider range of wavelengths, particularly at the infrared end of the light spectrum.

VDRs

I think it is true to say that VDRs (voltage dependent resistors) are now obsolete. They provide a resistance that decreases as the applied voltage is increased. The main application for components of this type was as a crude form of shunt type voltage stabiliser. They are probably little used these days, and are something I have not encountered for many years. Probably zener diodes offered higher performance at lower cost, rendering VDRs unnecessary. The cheapness of high quality monolithic voltage regulators has to a certain extent rendered ordinary zener diodes obsolete, and they seem to be relatively little used these days. One point in favour of VDRs is that, because they provide true resistance and are bipolar, they can operate with a.c. voltages as well as d.c. types.

Capacitors

Capacitors are another type of component that seems to be present in virtually every electronic circuit in large numbers. Whereas the number of different types of resistor in common use is quite limited, this is definitely not the case with capacitors. Look through a large electronic component catalogue and you are likely to find two dozen or more different types on offer. Such a wide range might seem to be unnecessarily complicating matters, and I suppose that some ranges do largely duplicate others. However, most capacitors are far from perfect, and a type that offers good performance in one respect often provides only poor or mediocre performance in one or more other respects. Selecting the right capacitor for the job is a matter of finding a type that has good performance in the areas that are important in your particular application. Often there will be several types that are suitable, and it is then a matter of choosing the type that is cheapest, or perhaps selecting the type which has the physical characteristics that you require.

A capacitor is a very simple type of component, and it takes the basic form shown in Figure 1.9. It is just two metal plates separated by a layer of insulation called the "dielectric". If a capacitor is connected to a battery or other voltage source, electrons flow from the negative terminal of the power source into the plate of the capacitor to which it connects. Similarly, electrons flow from the other plate into the positive terminal of the power source. How much current flows depends on the value of the capacitor, and the higher its value, the greater

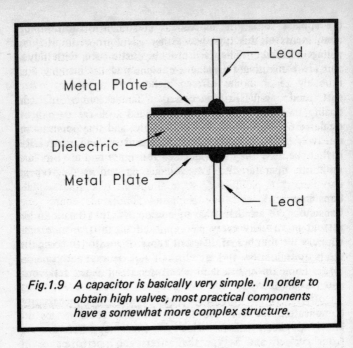

*Fig.1.9 A capacitor is basically very simple. In order to
obtain high valves, most practical components
have a somewhat more complex structure.*

the charge that will flow from the power source into the
battery. The value of the capacitor depends on the plate area,
the distance between the plates, and the quality of the
dielectric. Large plates, a narrow gap, and a high quality
dielectric provide high values.

If the power source is removed, the charge that flowed
into the capacitor will be retained. Placing a resistance
between the terminals of the capacitor will result in the excess
of electrons on one plate flowing into the other plate where
there is a deficit of electrons. In other words, the capacitor
will discharge through the resistor. This ability of a capacitor
to store electricity and release it again is exploited in supply
smoothing and decoupling applications. The rate at which a
capacitor charges and discharges depends on the source/load
resistance, and the value of the capacitor. This enables a
resistor and capacitor to act as a simple timing circuit,
another feature which is much exploited in practical circuits

(in R − C oscillators as well as in straightforward timing applications). Capacitors have other useful properties, such as acting as tuned circuits when used in conjunction with inductors, and effectively passing a.c. signals while blocking d.c. ones.

Capacitor values are expressed in farads, and a capacitor having a value of one farad would need a charge current of one amp for one second in order to give a charge potential of one volt. This is a very high value indeed, and most large capacitors have values expressed in microfarads (i.e. one millionth of a farad). Lower values are normally given in nanofarads or picofarads. One thousand picofarads equals one nanofarad, and one thousand nanofarads equals one microfarad. A capacitor having a value of (say) 10 nanofarads (10n) could have its value expressed as 0.01 microfarads (0.01μ) or 10000 picofarads (10000p). Figure 1.10 shows the circuit symbols for various types of capacitor. Each type, in all its common practical forms, is described in the following section of this chapter.

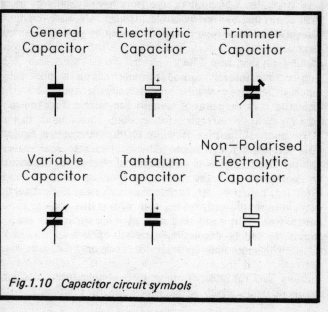

Fig.1.10 Capacitor circuit symbols

Practical Capacitors

Practical capacitors are not normally in the form of a couple of flat metal plates separated by a thin sheet of insulating material. Even moderate values of capacitance require large plates, and would be excessively large using this method of construction. The usual solution to the problem is to have two strips of metal foil interleaved with two layers of plastic foil, or some other insulating material. These are then rolled up tightly to give capacitors of the familiar cylindrical shape. Printed circuit mounting capacitors are often a sort of flat box-like shape, but in many cases they are still made in the same basic fashion. The strips of foil are folded over rather than rolled up, thus producing a rectangular and less rounded shape. Some capacitors (notably polycarbonate and physically similar types) have a slightly different method of construction, as shown in Figure 1.11. This is really just a variation on the standard "rolled-up" arrangement though.

Even with these methods of construction, and even if very thin pieces of foil are used, high value capacitors tend to be very large. In fact normal capacitors having values of more than about $2\mu2$ are not available. If high values are required, a slightly different type of capacitor must be used. This is the electrolytic type, which is readily available in values from about 470n to at least 4700μ.

The fundamental method of construction is not really much different to that of non-electrolytic types, but the dielectric is in the form of an absorbent material soaked in a liquid called "electrolyte" (in modern components this is often in the form of a jelly-like material and not a liquid). This enables very high values to be squashed into small spaces, but the price that has to be paid is that electrolytic capacitors are polarised. In other words, whereas an ordinary (non-polarised) capacitor can handle pure a.c. signals, electrolytic capacitors should only be fed with signals that contain a d.c. component. The main uses of high value capacitors are for supply smoothing, decoupling applications, and d.c. blocking, all of which normally provide the necessary d.c. polarising voltage.

Note that the polarity of an electrolytic capacitor is normally marked clearly on the body of the component with

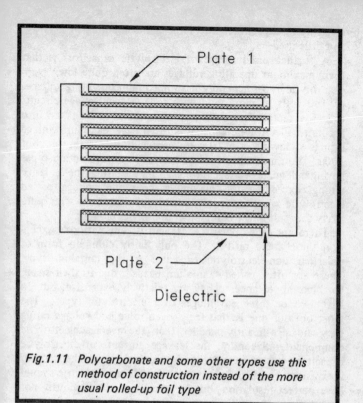

Fig.1.11 *Polycarbonate and some other types use this method of construction instead of the more usual rolled-up foil type*

"+" and (or) "−" signs, and that it is important that they should be connected into circuit the right way round. If an electrolytic capacitor is connected the wrong way round, particularly if it is a supply smoothing or decoupling type, quite a high current is likely to flow. This could easily result in the component exploding with a loud "crack" sound.

Electrolytic capacitors are widely available in both axial (horizontal mounting) and radial (vertical mounting) varieties. With the axial type the positive leadout wire is invariably indicated by an indentation around that end of the component's body, but the "+" and "−" signs are usually included as well. Note that there are actually special non-polarised electrolytic capacitors, but these are something of a rarity, and little used.

A further disadvantage of electrolytic capacitors is that their maximum operating voltages are often quite low. Non-electrolytic types generally have maximum operating voltages of 100 volts or more, and with today's low voltage circuits this is a factor that does not often have to be taken into account. Electrolytic capacitors often have maximum voltage ratings as low as 6 or 10 volts, especially values above about 100μ. You must therefore be careful to always obtain types having adequate voltage ratings. Like getting the polarity wrong, exceeding the maximum operating voltage of an electrolytic capacitor (or any other type come to that) is quite likely to result in the component literally exploding.

There are other polarised capacitors, but with one exception these are a rarity. The only fairly common form of polarised non-electrolytic capacitor is the tantalum type. These are often called "tantalum beads", due to their small, bead-like appearance. They are relatively expensive, but do have two or three advantages over electrolytic types. The most obvious one is that for a given value and voltage rating they are significantly smaller than the average electrolytic component. Secondly, the leakage currents of electrolytic capacitors are often quite high, particularly in the case of inexpensive and high value types. Ideally the dielectric should have perfect insulation, but in practice this is obviously not achievable. However, most non-electrolytic types have an insulation resistance of many tens of megohms at low to medium voltages. So high in fact, that for most practical purposes it can be regarded as infinite.

With electrolytic capacitors it is not uncommon for the leakage resistance to be just a few megohms, and in some cases it is less than 100k. This is adequate for non-critical applications such as supply smoothing and decoupling, but it is inadequate for applications such as C — R timing circuits, coupling, etc. The leakage levels of tantalum capacitors are normally adequate for timing circuits and other critical applications.

A further problem with electrolytic capacitors is that they mostly have very high tolerance figures. Figures of plus 50%

and minus 20% are not untypical, and I have encountered electrolytic capacitors having tolerances as high as plus 100% and minus 50%! Tantalum capacitors are not what could really be described as close tolerance components, but with a tolerance that is usually plus and minus 10% or 20% they are significantly better than most electrolytic types in this respect.

There is a slight drawback to tantalum capacitors which should not be overlooked. Although electrolytic capacitors should not be fed with voltages of the wrong polarity, they are often used in circuits where there is a definite possibility that they will be fed with a small reverse voltage. In practice this does not seem to matter too much, and these circuits seem to operate well and reliably. Many tantalum capacitors are very intolerant of reverse voltages, and should not be used in this manner.

Non-Electrolytic Types

There are a number of common types of non-electrolytic capacitor, and it is worth considering the different characteristics of the more popular types, and their applications. The largest category these days is the plastic foil type. These are types which have some form of plastic dielectric, and the most common types are polystyrene, polyester, Mylar, and polycarbonate components.

Polystyrene capacitors are good quality types suitable for use at high frequencies as well as in high quality audio equipment, computers, etc. They have good thermal stability, making them suitable for use in tuned circuits and other applications where stability is important. They are available in values from a few picofarads up to about 100n. The tolerance rating is usually 5% or 10%, but there are also high quality 1% types available. Polystyrene capacitors have extremely high leakage resistances.

Although polystyrene capacitors may seem like the ideal type for just about every application, they are less universal in their application than might at first appear to be the case. One slight problem is that they are relatively expensive, being around double the price of most other plastic foil capacitors. They also tend to be relatively large, with high values having perhaps five times the volume of comparable polyester and polycarbonate components. Very high values of about 120n to $2\mu2$ do not seem to be available, and would presumably be very large indeed by modern standards.

Where good stability and relatively low tolerance ratings are needed, and provided a component of the required value can be obtained, a polystyrene capacitor is likely to be the best choice. They are also a good choice where low value capacitors are required, since polystyrene capacitors of this type are usually quite small and reasonably inexpensive. They are not a good choice for general use at medium to high values.

You could be forgiven for thinking that polystyrene capacitors are polarised components, since many of them have one end of the body coloured red. They are quite definitely non-polarised, but this coloured end does have significance. Polystyrene capacitors are manufactured in such a way that one plate entirely surrounds the other one and shields it. The red marking indicates the leadout wire that connects to the outer plate. In an application such as the tuned circuit of an oscillator, the leadout wire indicated by the red marking would be the one that was connected to earth. This should then help to minimise problems with stray feedback, hand capacitance effects, etc. In something like a coupling or decoupling application, it is unlikely to make much difference which way round the component is connected (but if one leadout connects to earth, it is probably just as well to make this the one indicated by the red end of the component).

Polyester and Mylar capacitors are the ones that are mostly used as general purpose medium to high value (up to about $2\mu2$) components. They are small, reasonably inexpensive, have tolerance figures of about 5% to 20%, and are stable enough for most applications. Some critical applications require the greater stability and closer tolerance of high quality polystyrene capacitors, but such applications are few and far between. Polyester and Mylar components work well into the radio frequency range, but they are not normally used into the v.h.f. range.

Polycarbonate capacitors used to be featured in many component catalogues, but seem to be something of a rarity these days. They are generally somewhat more expensive than polyester and mylar types, but are somewhat superior in most respects. Probably for most amateur requirements the higher specification is of no consequence, and these capacitors have been dropped from the component catalogues in favour of the lower cost polyester and Mylar types.

Two relatively rare forms of capacitor are the metallised polypropylene and metallised polyethylene types. These are high quality components that are mainly designed for high voltage a.c. use (such as in mains suppression circuits). They are available in values from about 1n to 1μ. Due to their relatively large physical size and high cost they are normally only used in applications that require very high voltage ratings.

Ceramic capacitors have what are, on the face of it, very poor characteristics. Their tolerance values are mostly similar to those of electrolytic capacitors, they have poor temperature stability, and their value tends to change quite considerably with ageing. For most purposes they are considerably less than ideal. They do have advantages though, one of which is that they can be made physically quite small, even with values in the region of 100n to 470n. They are mostly quite cheap as well. Probably their most useful quality though, is that they operate well at frequencies into the u.h.f. spectrum. Their lack of stability renders them unsuitable for use in critical applications such as tuned circuits, but they are well suited to coupling and decoupling applications where changes in value are likely to be of no practical consequence.

Note that a fair percentage of the ceramic capacitors on offer have quite low maximum operating voltages. I have encountered miniature types having voltage rating as low as 3 volts. When ordering ceramic capacitors you therefore need to exercise a certain amount of care to ensure that you obtain components having adequate voltage ratings.

In general, it is best not to utilize ordinary ceramic capacitors in audio circuits, particularly the input stages of sensitive audio amplifiers. These components, when used in this way, can produce problems with microphony (i.e. they can tend to pick up vibration and produce corresponding electrical signals that are fed into the signal chain, producing "clunks" and "bangs" on the audio output).

Traditionally, ceramic capacitors have a disc-type shape, and they are often referred to as "disc ceramics". These days though, they are also available in box-type encapsulations, similar to the popular ranges of polyester capacitors. Some of these offer better tolerances and stability than ordinary disc ceramics, and are suitable for more demanding applications. They also pack quite high values into extremely small encapsulations, and are well suited to circuits that must be miniaturised.

Ceramic plate capacitors are a form of miniature ceramic capacitor. Many of these components only seem to be about two or three millimetres square by about 1 millimetre thick, making them about the smallest components in general use today. They are manufactured in values from about 1p up to at least 100n, but currently they only seem to be readily available in values up to about 10n. The higher values have similar characteristics to disc ceramic capacitors, and are used in the same sorts of application (h.f. and v.h.f. coupling and decoupling). The lower values have what are often quite close tolerances (about 2%), and although they do not offer the same sort of stability as high quality polystyrene capacitors, they are often used in tuned circuits where something less than the ultimate in performance is required.

At one time silvered mica capacitors (or or just plain "silver mica" capacitors as they are often called) were the standard choice for any application that required fairly low values. With the introduction of various plastic foil and ceramic types over the years, silvered mica types have tended to be used less and less. They still have excellent characteristics, with extremely good stability, making them well suited to critical applications such as tuned circuits in communications equipment. They have two main drawbacks, one of which is that they are not particularly small. Modern components are somewhat better in this respect than those of many years ago, but they are still substantially larger than most plastic foil types of comparable value and maximum operating voltage. Probably their main drawback though, is their relatively high cost. A 1n 5% silvered mica capacitor for example, is likely to cost about twice as much as a 1% polystyrene type, and about five times as much as a 5% polystyrene component. These capacitors are really only a worthwhile proposition in applications that genuinely require the level of performance they provide.

Colour Codes

Colour codes are used to some extent with capacitors, but their use is nothing like as widespread as it is for resistors. At one time colour codes on capacitors were much more widespread, but the codes that were once used on disc ceramic and tantalum bead capacitors are now well and truly obsolete. Most capacitors simply have the value written on in alpha-numeric characters, but the method of value marking can be a bit cryptic at times. In the case of plastic foil capacitors the value is often written on in the form that it normally appears on circuit diagrams (1n, 2µ2, 330p, etc.).

With some types of capacitor, notably many ceramic types, the method of value marking is less obvious. You will often encounter a marking such as "332", which at first sight makes the value something less than obvious. In fact this indicates a value of 3n3. This system operates in a fashion which is similar to resistor colour coding, with the first two digits simply showing the first two digits of the value. The third digit is the multiplier, and you simply add the indicated number of zeros to the first two digits. In the example given earlier, the first two digits of the value are "33", and two zeros must be added to this. The total value is therefore 3300, and it is in picofarads. This gives a final value of 3300p, or 3n3 in other words.

The values on low value ceramic capacitors can sometimes look a little odd as the leading zero is often omitted, and the values are often given in nanofarads rather than picofarads. A marking such as "n27" therefore indicates a value of 0.27 nanofarads, or 270p. Ceramic plate capacitors often have a coloured top, and this is apparently not there for decorative purposes! It actually indicates the temperature coefficient of the component. A list of colours and the temperature coefficients they represent are provided on page 32.

Although the relatively poor temperature stability of many ceramic capacitors is normally considered a drawback, it can be advantageous in some applications. The change in value with temperature of a ceramic capacitor can be used to compensate for changes in other components, thus giving lower

Colour	Temperature Coefficient
Black	Zero
Orange	−150 ppm/degree C.
Violet	−750 ppm/degree C.
Yellow	medium K
Green	high K

levels of drift.

The tolerance of a capacitor is often left unmarked. The maximum operating voltage is more likely to be included, and I suppose that this could reasonably be regarded as more important than the tolerance. In some instances the tolerance is indicated by a code letter. This system operates in the same manner as the tolerance coding of resistors that have the value marked using alpha-numeric characters. Refer to the section of this chapter dealing with resistors for a list of code letters/tolerances.

Although colour codes are little used on capacitors these days, there is one type where they are still used to a significant extent. This is the C280 polyester type (or similar). In fact not all capacitors of this style are colour coded these days, and a fair percentage simply have the value and maximum operating voltage written onto the top surface of the case. However, there are still significant numbers of colour coded C280 capacitors in circulation, and due to the popularity of these components you are quite likely to encounter them fairly regularly.

Figure 1.12 helps to explain the way in which this method of colour coding operates. It has similarities to the standard method of resistor colour coding, and the first three bands (i.e. the top three) indicate the value in the normal way. The first two bands indicate the first two digits, while the third band shows the multiplier value. As an example, if the first three bands are black, brown, and yellow, this indicates initial digits of "10", and a multiplier of 10000 (i.e. add four zeros). This gives a total value of 100000p, 100n, or 0.1μ, depending on your preferred units of measurement.

The fourth and fifth bands respectively indicate the tolerance and maximum operating voltages, using the method of

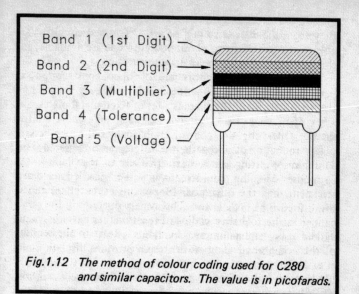

Fig.1.12 *The method of colour coding used for C280 and similar capacitors. The value is in picofarads.*

colour coding detailed below.

Colour	Tolerance	Voltage
Black	20%	—
White	10%	—
Green	5%	—
Orange	2.5%	—
Red	2%	250V
Brown	1%	—
Yellow	—	400V

Thus, a capacitor which has white and red as its fourth and fifth bands has a tolerance of 10% and a maximum operating voltage of 250 volts.

Variables and Trimmers

A few types of variable capacitor are available, but with current technology it is not practical to produce high value types. The main use of variable capacitors is as tuning controls in radio receivers and other radio frequency equipment where they form the capacitive half of a L – C tuned circuit. Variable capacitors of up to about 500p in value are available, and this is adequate for tuning control applications.

Many variable capacitors are of open construction, or have transparent plastic casings, making it easy to see how they operate. Basically there is a set of fixed metal plates, and a set of moving plates operated via the spindle and a control knob. Operating the control knob enables the two sets of plates to be meshed together to a greater or lesser degree. This gives control over the effective size of the plates in the capacitor. Meshing them to a large extent gives a large effective plate area and a high capacity – unmeshing them gives a low effective plate area, and a low capacity.

The highest quality variable capacitors are the air spaced variety. As their name suggests, there is only air between the plates, and the air gap between them provides insulation and acts as the dielectric. Components of this type usually have ball bearings to provide very smooth and precise operation. They are necessarily built and set up with a fairly high degree of precision, and need to be treated carefully. Any slight maladjustment and the two sets of plates will short circuit together. Similarly, any rough treatment could easily result in one of the plates becoming bent, again resulting in the two sets of plates short circuiting together at some settings of the component.

Variable capacitors of the solid dielectric type are generally somewhat less stable and precise than the air-spaced variety, but are usually much lower in cost. Their general method of construction is similar to that of air-spaced types, but sheets of a plastic insulating material are used to hold the two sets of plates apart. This enables very small gaps to be used between the plates with no risk of them short circuiting to one another. The plates themselves are often very thin and something less than rigid. This enables components of reasonably high value to be condensed into quite a small volume, and to be produced at relatively low prices. For something like the tuning control in a high quality short wave communications receiver the greater stability and precision of an air-spaced component is called for, but in less critical applications (such

34

as medium and long wave broadcast radios) a solid dielectric type should be perfectly adequate.

Variable capacitors often have as many as three or even four gangs. In other words, there are several sections that are all controlled by a common shaft. Sometimes each section is of the same value, but it is quite common for each gang to have a different value. One reason for this is that many two gang components are designed for operation in medium and long wave radios. The section used to tune the oscillator stage (which is usually the rear section) operates over a much higher frequency range than the section which controls the r.f. tuning. Accordingly, the oscillator section has a somewhat lower value in order to prevent it from covering too wide a frequency range. In practice a fixed value capacitor (the "padder" capacitor) is often used in series with the oscillator section in order to effectively adjust its value to precisely the required figure.

Another reason for having sections of different values is that many variable capacitors are intended for operation in a.m./f.m. radios. The f.m. section of the set operates in the v.h.f. range and only requires very low values of capacitance swing, necessitating separate gangs for the a.m. and f.m. sections of the radio. A typical variable capacitor for use in an a.m./f.m. radio would have four gangs, with something like 220p/175p sections for the a.m. circuits, and 20p/20p for the f.m. circuits. Note that the sections of an f.m. tuning capacitor are normally the same. This is because the frequency ranges covered by the r.f. and oscillator tuned circuit are similar (but not identical). A padder capacitor can effectively reduce the value of the oscillator gang slightly, if necessary.

Preset capacitors (which are often called "trimmers") are usually in the form of miniature air-spaced or solid dielectric components having adjusting screws rather than standard spindles. These mostly operate in the same way as variable types, but there is one exception in the form of compression trimmers. These are a form of solid dielectric capacitor, but they are designed so that under normal circumstances the two sets of plates tend to spring apart, giving a significant air gap between them. The value of a capacitor is governed by a number of factors, one of which is the distance between the two plates (or sets of plates). The smaller the gap, the higher the capacitance. A compression trimmer has an adjustment screw which can be used to press the two sets of plates closer together, giving an increase in capacitance. The minimum capacitance of this type of trimmer tends to be relatively high, but the capacitance swing obtained is wide enough for most applications. This type of trimmer is mainly used where a high maximum capacitance is required, and values up to about 500p are produced.

Trimmer capacitors are often built into variable capacitors, and connected in parallel with them internally. These trimmers are often in the form of miniature air spaced types, but other arrangements are used, including crude but quite effective compression trimmers.

Although fixed value capacitors are manufactured in the usual E24 and E12 series of values, note that trimmer capacitors come in a variety of capacitance ranges. It should perhaps be mentioned that fixed value capacitors are often only available in a limited range of values, known as the E6 series. This is effectively every other value in the E12 series (1.0, 1.5, 2.2, 3.3, 4.7, and 6.8).

Inductors

In its most basic form an inductor consists of a piece of wire wound around a former of some kind. The former can be a plastic tube or a solid rod of plastic, but in most cases it is made of ferrite or some other dust-iron material. The point of using a ferrite core is that it reduces the number of turns required for a given inductance. An ideal inductor would have zero resistance, but in practice there will always be a certain amount of resistance through the winding. The quality of an inductor is expressed as a "Q" value, and the higher the quality of the component, the greater its Q value. In order to obtain a high Q the winding should have as few turns as possible, and by enabling fewer turns for a given inductance to be used, a ferrite core gives increased Q value.

Although a coil of wire may not seem to provide any electrical qualities other than pure resistance, matters are by no means as straightforward as this. When a power source is connected to an inductor, a magnetic field is generated around the component. The effect of this rising magnetic field is to induce an electric current in the coil of wire, but this current is of the opposite polarity to the power source. Consequently, it opposes the flow of current from the power source. With a small inductor the current through the component will quickly rise to a level limited only by the source resistance of the power source and the resistance through the inductor itself. With a very large inductor having a great many turns, the influence of the rising magnetic field will be quite large, and it will take a significant length of time for the current to build up to a high level.

The basic unit of inductance is the henry, and with a component of one henry in value, an input potential of one volt results in a rise in current of one amp per second. In practice a value of one henry is pretty massive, and most inductors are only a tiny fraction of a henry. The values of most inductors are therefore expressed in either microhenries (one millionth of a henry) or millihenries (one thousandth of a henry).

An inductor has properties which could be regarded as the inverse of those of a capacitor. It passes d.c. signals but resists a.c. ones. The higher the input frequency, the more an inductor resists the signal. A capacitor has a reactance figure that decreases with increased input frequency. In common with a capacitor, it is capable of storing an electric charge. When a power source is disconnected from an inductor the magnetic field around it collapses. This collapsing field generates a voltage across the inductor. Unlike a capacitor, the charge is given up when the voltage source is removed, rather than when a load is connected across the component. In practical applications the properties of an inductor tend to be less useful than those of a capacitor, and inductors are found in few circuits in any numbers. In fact it is probably true to say that they are totally absent from the majority of electronic circuits.

Figure 1.13 shows the circuit symbols for various types of inductor. The winding of an inductor is not always indicated by a series of semicircles, and the two main alternatives are a sort of multiple loop and a simple solid box shape. However, the style shown in Figure 1.13 is the most common form of

37

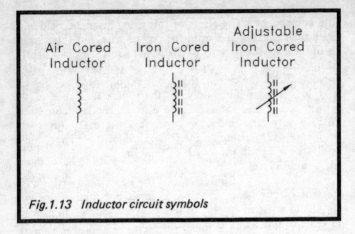

Air Cored
Inductor

Iron Cored
Inductor

Adjustable
Iron Cored
Inductor

Fig.1.13 Inductor circuit symbols

inductor symbol.

Inductors are found most frequently in radio frequency circuits, and in this context they are often called r.f. chokes. It is important to realise that these low cost inductors are only intended for use at radio frequencies, which in practice generally means about 100kHz or more. In theory it does not matter what signal frequency an r.f. choke is subjected to, it will always operate equally efficiently. In reality the situation tends to be somewhat different. As already explained, most inductors are wound on some form of dust iron core which gives increased Q value by permitting fewer turns to be used for a given inductance. The effect of these cores can be enormous. However, the core will only be efficient over a certain frequency range, and is likely to be far less effective at low frequencies than at frequencies well into the radio frequency range. The practical consequence of this is that these components have lower values at low frequencies than they do at high frequencies.

Another important limitation to keep in mind when dealing with small r.f. chokes is that they are only intended to handle small currents. For the higher value r.f. chokes the maximum operating current can be as low as 25 milliamps. The reason for this limitation is mainly that the component is wound using a large number of turns of very thin wire. This produces

38

quite a significant resistance, and results in the component dissipating too much power and overheating at more than modest current flows. One factor, but usually a minor one in practice, is that the core materials tend to become saturated at high currents and cease to work efficiently. However, current flows of at least a few hundred milliamps are normally needed before core saturation is likely to become a significant factor.

The values of r.f. chokes are mainly just written on the components, with a code letter perhaps being used to denote the tolerance rating. Some recent chokes seem to have colour codes, but these should not give any difficulties. In essence, this colour coding is exactly the same as the four band resistor type. The only difference is that the value is in microhenries instead of ohms. Divide the value by 1000 to obtain an answer in millihenries, or by 1000000 for an answer in henries.

Adjustable r.f. inductors are available, and are normally in the form of a plastic former and base contained in an aluminium screening can and fitted with an adjustable dust iron core. The screening can, provided it is suitably earthed, will prevent the coil from radiating a strong signal, or from picking up signals. The core usually has a slit or a hexagonal hole into which a matching trimming tool can be fitted. The interior of the former and the outside of the core have matching screw threads, so that the core can be screwed into and out of the former. As the core is adjusted down into the coil, it effectively increases its value, and gives an increase in the inductance of the component as well. Note that some variable inductors are intended for use at v.h.f., and have cores which are only likely to give the desired effect over the v.h.f. range. These often lack the screening can.

Going to Pot

Inductors seem to be used relatively little in audio frequency circuits. A major factor here is that low frequency applications tend to require relatively high values, which in turn means using large numbers of turns. This results in components that are quite large and expensive by current standards. Probably the main use for low frequency inductors is in cross-over networks for multi-driver hi-fi loudspeakers. Due to the fairly high currents involved, these are wound using heavy gauges of wire, and for efficiency they are often wound on laminated iron formers (similar to those used for mains transformers). Since hi-fi loudspeakers, even the smaller types, are quite bulky and heavy, the size of the components in the cross-over networks is not a major problem.

Another common use for low frequency inductors is in mains suppression filters. The most simple types of filter make use of three capacitors and no inductors, but the more complex types mostly use at least two inductors. These components are normally wound on a special type of ferrite core called a "toroid". This is basically just a ring of a suitable ferrite material. Toroidal inductors are also used in many switch mode power supplies incidentally.

For the ultimate in performance at low frequencies a pot core is used as the basis of an inductor. Pot cores vary somewhat in their exact shape, but are mostly quite elaborate. The term "core" is perhaps a little misleading, as these components fit around the coil of wire as well as inside it. To make this possible a pot core is in two halves (top and bottom), and the coil is wound on a matching bobbin. This bobbin fits onto the lower former, and then the top half of the coil is lowered into and over it. The two halves of the core can be glued together, or metal clips can be used to hold them together. Some pot cores have an adjustable core that can be fitted into a hole down the centre of the component. This enables the value to be adjusted over a limited but useful range of values.

Inductors wound on pot cores can achieve quite high Q values even at fairly low frequencies. These components are something less than popular though, and do have a few drawbacks. One of these is simply the cost. Ready-made inductors wound on high quality pot cores are not easy to obtain, and are likely to cost several pounds each even if a source of supply can be traced. Due to these supply problems it is often necessary to resort to home wound coils, but even these are likely to be quite expensive to produce, especially if a large pot core is required. The pot cores themselves are not particularly tough. This is due to them being made from ferrite materials, which are not only extremely hard but also quite brittle. If you drop a pot core from a few feet onto a hard floor it will almost certainly smash into a large number of pieces and be rendered totally unusable.

Transformers

A transformer is basically just two inductors in close proximity to one another. Coupling an a.c. signal into one inductor results in it generating a varying magnetic field. As the magnetic lines of force of this field cut through the winding in the other inductor, they generate a signal in it. At very high frequencies, two simple inductors in close proximity might provide a reasonably efficient transformer. At lower frequencies though, getting an efficient coupling from one winding to the next is more difficult. In general, the lower the operating frequency, the more difficult it is to obtain a reasonably efficient coupling.

Figure 1.14 shows the circuit symbols for a range of transformer types. These are basically just the corresponding inductor circuit symbols, but with two or more windings being shown on opposite sides of a common core.

An important characteristic of a transformer is its turns ratio. In theory, if there are (say) 10 turns on the input ("primary") winding of a transformer, and 5 turns on its output ("secondary") winding, the output voltage will be half the input voltage. The output voltage is equal to the input voltage multiplied by the primary turns, and then divided by the number of secondary turns. If the secondary winding has more turns than the primary winding, there will be a voltage step-up through the component. A transformer does not provide true amplification though, and a step-up in voltage is matched by a corresponding step-down in maximum output current. With a two to one voltage step-up for example, the maximum output current is limited to half the input current. Similarly, with a two to one voltage step-down, the output current can be up to double the input current. Of course, this all assumes 100% efficiency, which in practice is not achieved. The output power can never exceed the input power, and in practice will normally be significantly less.

Mains transformers are one of the most common forms of transformer. A component of this type normally provides two functions. One is to provide safety isolation. Remember that

41

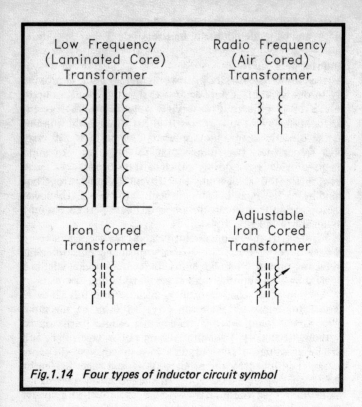

Fig.1.14 *Four types of inductor circuit symbol*

there is no direct connection from the primary winding to the secondary winding of a mains transformer. Consequently, you should not be able to obtain a shock from a low voltage secondary winding on a mains transformer. Of course, if the mains transformer has a high voltage secondary winding, you can sustain an electric shock by coming into contact with both terminals of the secondary winding. The second function is to convert the mains voltage to one that is more appropriate to the particular application concerned. With most modern circuits operating on quite low supply voltages, this usually means a secondary voltage of only about 5 to 30 volts.

42

Transformers are also used to process signals in audio and radio frequency equipment. In this context they operate as impedance matching devices. At one time transformers were often used at the output of amplifiers to provide an output impedance that matched the loudspeaker in use. They were even used for interstage coupling in many circuits. It is rare to find them used in either of these applications these days. With semiconductors it is not difficult to produce transformerless audio circuits, including power amplifiers that will drive standard 8 ohm impedance loudspeakers, and there are good reasons for doing so. Audio frequency transformers tend to be quite large and expensive. Also, they often provide levels of performance that fall well short of perfection. They can introduce amplitude distortion and irregularities in the frequency response of the circuit.

When used as an impedance matching device, the step-up or down in impedance is not the same as the turns ratio. It is equal to the square of the turns ratio. As an example, if a transformer has an input impedance of 100R and a turns ratio of 1 to 9, squaring 9 gives an impedance ratio of 81 to 1. Multiplying the input impedance of 100R by 81 gives the output impedance, which is 8100R, or 8k1 in other words.

Radio frequency transformers are used a great deal, and usually have at least one winding as a tuned type. In other words, it is connected in parallel with a capacitor so that it functions as a tuned circuit. Apart from providing impedance matching, the transformer plus tuning capacitor then provides bandpass filtering as well. Tuned r.f. transformers are much used in the r.f., mixer, oscillator, and intermediate frequency stages of radio receivers.

Practical Transformers
Radio frequency transformers (including intermediate frequency types) are usually very much like adjustable r.f. inductors, but with two windings on a single former. Transformers, whether for r.f. use or otherwise, often have tappings on one or both of their windings. In other words, there are connections at some point or points along the winding, as well as at the ends. Physically, r.f. transformers used to be available in a variety of shapes and sizes. These days they are still

available in different sizes, but they are virtually all in the form of printed circuit mounting components contained in rectangular aluminium screening cans. The type normally used by electronics hobbyists have 10 millimetre screening cans, but the 7 millimetre type are sometimes used.

Radio frequency transformers are not normally sold on the basis of some form of value. They are invariably designed for a specific purpose such as a medium wave oscillator coil, or a 455kHz first i.f. transformer, and are sold as such. In the case of i.f. transformers, and a few other types, the necessary tuning capacitance is included as an internal part of the component. Virtually all r.f. transformers are fitted with adjustable dust-iron cores for alignment purposes.

Mains transformers are usually wound on a laminated metal core which gives good efficiency at the low mains frequency of 50Hz. The efficiency may still not be terribly good, with perhaps up to 70% of the input signal finding its way to the output. When operated at maximum output current it is normal for mains transformers to run quite warm, or even hot in some cases. Most mains transformers now take the form shown in Figure 1.15. Like most low frequency transformer cores, in order to improve efficiency the core actually fits around the windings to some extent, as well as going down the middle.

In days gone by it was normal for the primary winding to be placed onto the bobbin first, with the secondary winding or windings being placed on top of it. These days the standard arrangement is this split or twin bobbin arrangement, with one taking the primary winding, and the other taking the secondary or secondaries. I think that I am correct in stating that the new method of construction has nothing to do with gaining improved efficiency. It is more a matter of getting the primary and secondary windings physically well separated, so that there is no realistic risk of the insulation between them breaking down and the mains supply finding a direct route through the component. It is purely a safety measure.

Toroidal mains transformers have been available for a number of years now, and they are wound on a ring-like core. This permits increased efficiency to be obtained. The advantage of this is not primarily the reduced power consumption it

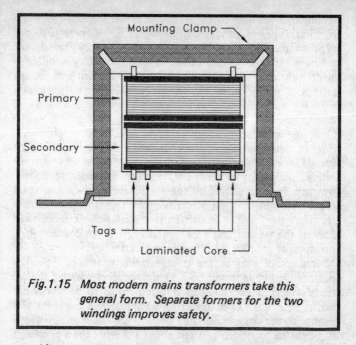

Fig.1.15 Most modern mains transformers take this general form. Separate formers for the two windings improves safety.

provides, or even the reduced heat generation. The main advantage of toroidal mains transformers is that they are physically much smaller and lighter than conventional components of similar ratings. An added bonus is that the stray magnetic field generated around the component is usually very much weaker than that from a comparable conventional component. This is useful for mains transformers that will be used in the power supplies of sensitive audio and test equipment.

Mains transformer ratings can cause a certain amount of confusion to the uninitiated. The main point to bear in mind is that the secondary voltage and current ratings are a.c. and not d.c. ratings. The fact that a transformer has a secondary current rating of 2 amps for example, does not mean that it can be used in a power supply that will provide an output of up to 2 amps d.c. In most cases it will provide less than this. The exception is where a power supply uses a centre-tapped secondary winding with push-pull rectification (the two rectifier type). Although it might at first appear that this type of rectification offers very good efficiency, this is not actually the case. The centre tapped secondary winding is effectively two windings of the required current and voltage ratings, wired in series. It therefore takes, for instance, two 9 volt 1 amp secondary windings to provide a 9 volt d.c. 1 amp output.

In the case of a bridge rectifier (the type which uses a ring of four rectifiers) the maximum d.c. output current should be no more than 0.62 of the transformer's a.c. current rating. As this type needs only a single, untapped secondary winding. it is actually a bit more efficient than the push-pull type. A simple half wave rectifier (the type that uses a single rectifier) gives a d.c. output current that is little more than 25% of the transformer's a.c. current rating. Understandably, this type of rectifier is little used in practice.

Remember that as the voltage rating is an a.c. type, the peak output voltage will be 1.41 times higher. With practical transformers under no load it often seems to be somewhat higher than this. Consequently, the unloaded d.c. output of a mains power supply circuit, even with the voltage drops through the rectifiers, is often about 1.5 times the a.c. voltage rating of the mains transformer. Under full load though, the d.c. output voltage usually drops to a voltage not much in excess of the mains transformer's secondary voltage rating.

In component catalogues you may sometimes come across "autotransformers". These are used either to step up a foreign mains supply of about 110 volts to 240 volts so that it can operate with U.K. mains equipment, or to step-down the 240 volt U.K. mains supply to about 110 volts so that it can be used with equipment intended for operation on foreign supplies of this potential. Autotransformers have a single but tapped winding which is used in the manner shown in Figure 1.16(a). This is equivalent to the circuit of Figure 1.16(b). The position of the tapping, controls the step-up/down ratio. There is no isolation between the input and the output, but this does not matter as the equipment fed from the transformer should include safety isolation of some type.

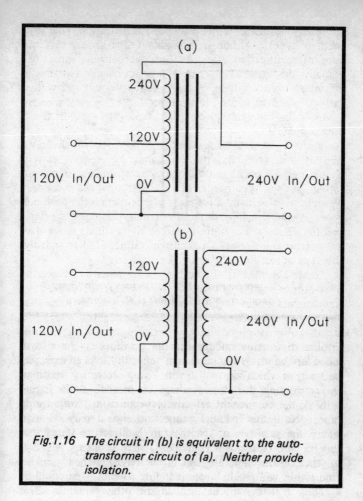

Fig.1.16 The circuit in (b) is equivalent to the auto-
transformer circuit of (a). Neither provide
isolation.

For maximum versatility, many modern mains transformers have twin 120 volt primary windings. These are connected in parallel for operation on 120 volt mains supplies, or in series for use with the 240 volt U.K. mains. Figure 1.17 shows the correct method of connection for operation with a 240 volt supply.

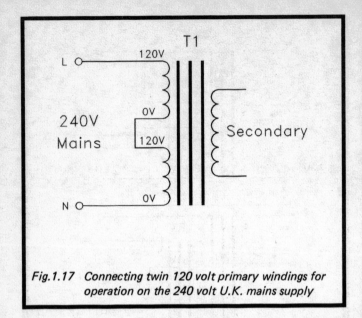

Fig.1.17 Connecting twin 120 volt primary windings for operation on the 240 volt U.K. mains supply

Similarly, many modern mains transformers have twin secondary windings for maximum versatility. As an example, take a type which has twin 6 volt 1 amp secondary windings. By connecting the two windings in parallel, as in Figure 1.18(a), the component effectively becomes a 6 volt 2 amp type. Note that parallel connection should only be used where the retailer's or manufacturer's literature states that this method of use is acceptable. If the secondary windings of the transformer are not accurately matched, parallel connection will result in one winding forcing what could be a pretty massive current through the other winding. This could easily result in the component rapidly overheating.

Connecting the secondary windings in series, as in Figure 1.18(b), gives a 12 volt 1 amp output. Note that it must be a "6V" and a "0V" terminal that are wired together, not two "0V" or two "6V" types. There will be no damage if you link two terminals of the same type, but the two windings will then cancel one another out, giving zero output voltage.

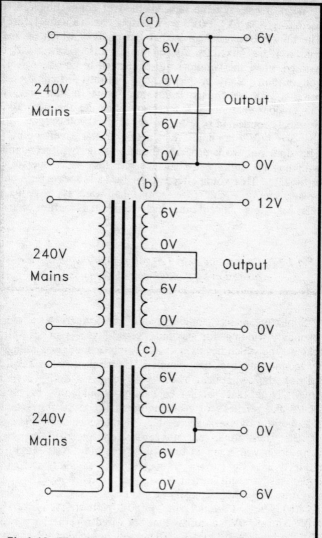

Fig.1.18 Three ways of using a mains transformer having twin (matched) secondary windings

What is basically the same method of connection can be used to give a 6V − 0V − 6V output, as in Figure 1.18(c). The only difference here is that the point at which the two windings are linked is utilized in this case, whereas it is ignored when the windings are connected to give a single 12 volt output. Many people seem to run into difficulty when using a twin secondary mains transformer in this way, as the obvious method of connection is to use the two "0V" terminals connected together to act as the 0 volt output, with the two "6V" terminals then acting as the 6 volt outputs. This does not work properly though, as the two secondaries will then be working in-phase whereas they must operate in anti-phase. This would effectively reduce a full-wave push-pull power supply circuit to a simple half-wave type, giving a relatively low current and high ripple d.c. output signal.

Chapter 2

SEMICONDUCTORS

I should think that one of the most confusing aspects of electronics for newcomers to the hobby is the vast range of semiconductors that are currently available. Not only is there a wide range of different types available (diodes, transistors, thyristors, integrated circuits, etc.), there are vast numbers of devices within each category listed in component catalogues. I would guesstimate that the larger electronic component retailers list in excess of one thousand different semiconductor devices.

Although there is a vast array of semiconductor devices on offer, the number of different types in common use is relatively small. With a little effort it is not too difficult to familiarise yourself with the main types, their important characteristics, etc. The number of components available within most categories is quite large, but they all provide the same basic function. One device might be designed to work well in low level audio circuits, another might have characteristics that are optimised for very high frequency use, and another might be intended for high power use. Although there are in many cases numerous sub-groups within each category of semiconductors, in reality there is an enormous amount of overlap. Retailers' lists of transistors in particular, tend to contain masses of largely interchangeable components. In some cases the same transistor is available under several different type numbers, with the only difference between each one being the encapsulation and (or) leadout configuration!

In this chapter we will consider the main categories of semiconductor, and will also look into the various types within each category. This should help newcomers to electronics to understand the masses of data and terminology found in the semiconductors section of most electronic component catalogues. Space does not permit details of every component to be given, but in most cases this is not really necessary. If you can understand the semiconductor data in catalogues, you can sort out which devices are likely to be suitable for a given application.

One aspect of semiconductors that should ideally be considered on a device by device basis is integrated circuits. However, there are so many different types performing so many different functions that this is not possible in a book of this size. In fact, in order to detail all the integrated circuits in common use these days would take several large books. Integrated circuits are covered in Chapter 3, and by necessity are only considered in fairly broad terms. This should still be sufficient to help you "decipher" most of the integrated circuit jargon to be found in electronic component catalogues.

Valves

The most simple form of semiconductor is the diode. The circuit symbols for various types of diode are shown in Figure 2.1. There seems to be some variation in the diode

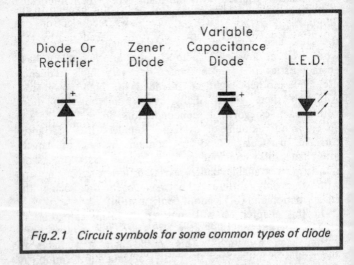

Fig.2.1 Circuit symbols for some common types of diode

symbol, and although the triangle in the symbols of Figure 2.1 are shown filled in, sometimes they are only shown in outline. Another variation (but a rare one) is to have a circle around the standard diode symbol. There are further variations in the markings of the terminals. These are not strictly necessary, since the symbol itself makes the polarity of the component quite clear. However, the cathode terminal is, somewhat confusingly perhaps, often marked with a "+" sign. Apparently, this method of marking indicates the terminal from which a positive going signal will emerge from the component. An alternative form of marking is for the anode and cathode to be marked "a" and "k" respectively. Presumably "k" is used instead of "c", as the latter could be confused with capacitor identification markings.

The basic action of a diode is very simple, and it merely allows a flow of current in one direction, but blocks any flow of current in the other direction. It is a sort of electronic valve in other words, and a semiconductor diode does in fact provide the same function as a basic vacuum tube type electronic valve diode of days gone by.

The basic way in which an old vacuum tube device operates is reasonably easy to understand. The cathode electrode is heated, causing the electronics in it to become excited to the point where they leave the cathode. The freed electrons can be attracted towards another electrode placed nearby (the anode) if it is made positive with respect to the cathode. In other words, connecting a supply to the device with the positive supply connected to the anode and the negative supply lead going to the cathode, causes an electric current to flow. A current flow is not possible in the opposite direction, since the anode is cold and will not produce free electronics that can be attracted towards the cathode.

Amplification is possible if an extra electrode is placed between the cathode and the anode. This electrode is in the form of a wire mesh. The voltage fed to this electrode will, depending on its polarity and amplitude, encourage a flow of electrons from the cathode to the anode, giving a lower resistance through the component, virtually shut off the current flow, or anything between these two extremes. This gives amplification because a low power signal applied this extra electrode (the "grid") can control a much higher power in the anode circuit. I suppose that strictly speaking the input signal is not being amplified, but is being used to generate a higher power version of itself. The effect is much the same as if the input signal was genuinely being enlarged though, and the indirect means by which amplification is achieved is largely of academic importance.

Semiconductor Diodes

If considered in detail, the theory of semiconductors is quite involved and, quite frankly, far from easy to fully understand. This book is not primarily concerned with the theoretical side of things, and so we will not dwell on this aspect of semiconductors. Basically, a diode consists of two pieces of semiconductor material. In the early days of "solid state" devices this usually meant two pieces of germanium, but modern devices are mostly based on silicon. The two pieces of semiconductor material are not identical, and have small amounts of different impurities added. The amounts involved are very small indeed, being of the order of one part in ten million. The impurities are called "dopants" incidentally. The semiconductor materials must have an extremely high level of purity prior to the addition of the dopants. Getting raw materials of suitable purity was a major problem in the early days of semiconductor manufacture, and with the even more stringent requirements for many modern components, it remains problematic.

There are two types of semiconductor material called "N" type and "P" type. These names are abbreviations for negative and positive respectively, and refer to the type of charge carriers in the material. Typical dopants are arsenic to produce N type material, and boron to produce P type semiconductor.

As the name suggests, semiconductor materials conduct to some extent, but are not such good conductors as metals. An electric current can therefore be passed through a piece of P type material, or through a piece of N type semiconductor. The situation is very different in cases where two pieces of semiconductor of different types have been fused together. What is called the "depletion layer" is formed at the junction of the two pieces of semiconductor material. This is basically a section where there is a shortage of the free electrons needed for conduction, giving a narrow layer of material that has a very high resistance.

On the face of it, a P-N semiconductor junction will not pass a significant current with an input signal of either polarity. In practice this is true, but only if the applied voltages are very low. With a bias voltage of the right polarity, silicon junctions will conduct reasonably well at voltages of more than about 0.5 to 0.7 volts. For germanium junctions the forward threshold potential is much lower, at typically around 0.1 to 0.2 volts. If the supply polarity is reversed, rather than causing the depletion layer to disappear, the applied signal actually causes it to get wider. This gives a very high reverse resistance. A high voltage will cause the component to break down and pass a high current. Normally the reverse voltage is kept below the breakdown figure, but as we shall see later, this reverse breakdown is put to good use in the form of zener diodes.

An ideal diode would have zero resistance when forward biased, regardless of the applied voltage. Its reverse resistance would be infinite. Failing that, the forward resistance would at least be low and identical at all input voltages, with the reverse resistance being extremely high. Practical semiconductor diodes tend to be far from perfect. The reverse resistance of silicon diodes is usually very high indeed, being a few hundred megohms or more in most cases. For most practical purposes this can be regarded as infinite, and silicon diodes perform well in this respect. Germanium diodes tend to be far less impressive as far as reverse resistances are concerned, and can usually only manage a reverse resistance of a few hundred kilohms. In some cases the reverse resistance is under one hundred kilohms. This obviously renders these components unsuitable for some applications.

The forward characteristic of semiconductor diodes tends to be far from perfect for both germanium and silicon components. As already explained, a certain threshold voltage has to be reached before a semiconductor diode will conduct significantly. This gives a severely non-linear forward bias characteristic, particularly in the case of silicon components. Again, this makes them unsuitable for some applications, or necessitates the use of extra circuitry in order to compensate for their shortcomings. Figure 2.2 shows typical transfer characteristics for both silicon and germanium diodes.

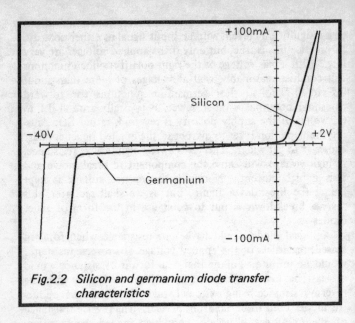

Fig.2.2 Silicon and germanium diode transfer characteristics

Manufacturing semiconductor components is a very complex process. It does not usually take the form of manufacturing N type and P type materials, and then fusing them together. Looking at things in highly over-simplified terms, the basic process is to first produce a large ingot of N type semiconductor material by growing it from a seed crystal. In this context, large means a piece of material that is often only about 50 millimetres or so in diameter. The ingot is cut into thin slices, or "wafers" as they are termed, using a diamond coated saw. The wafers are heated, and P type dopants are introduced. This produces a layer of P type semiconductor material on top of the N type base, or "substrate" as it is called. Further processing provides insulating layers to protect the semiconductor material, and to permit metal contacts to be made to it. Finally of course, it is diced up into thousands of individual diodes. These are usually mounted in glass encapsulations, complete with axial style leadout wires.

There are variations on this basic scheme of things. Germanium diodes are the main ones, and are produced using a simple masking process. A graphite disc containing numerous minute holes is placed over the wafer of germanium. Even more minute balls of aluminium (a P type dopant) are placed into the holes. Sufficient heat to just melt the aluminium is applied, after which leads are attached, the slice of germanium is diced up, and the individual diodes are mounted in glass encapsulations.

Practical Diodes

Although large numbers of different types of diode are produced, relatively few seem to be listed in most component catalogues. This is probably because a few general purpose diodes can satisfy most needs. Most designs for the electronics hobbyist only use one or two devices from about half a dozen popular types. For most purposes the ubiquitous 1N4148 will suffice. This is a general purpose silicon diode. For applications that require a low forward voltage drop, a germanium device such as the popular OA90 and OA91 is usually a better choice. A point to keep in mind when using germanium devices (both diodes and transistors) is that they are more vulnerable to heat damage than silicon devices. I have never found it necessary to use a heat-shunt when soldering these components into circuit, but the connections need to be completed fairly swiftly so that there is little time for the heat from the iron to pass along the leadout wire to the semiconductor material.

When is a diode not a diode? — when it is a rectifier! The term rectifier tends to confuse beginners at electronics. How does it differ from an ordinary diode? There is no real difference between diodes and rectifiers, but the term diode is normally used for a low power type, whereas a rectifier is normally accepted to be a component that will handle relatively high powers. I do not know of any hard and fast dividing line, but the smallest rectifiers seem to be designed to take currents of up to 1 amp. A realistic dividing line would therefore be at this figure.

On the face of it, there is little point in producing diodes and rectifiers, when a rectifier will operate perfectly well at low currents. In practice matters are not as simple as this. In many applications a rectifier can be used in place of a diode without any significant change in performance. However, there are some applications, particularly those that require high switching speeds, where a rectifier will not operate well. When a suitable forward bias is applied to a diode, the depletion layer disappears and it starts to conduct, but the depletion layer takes a small amount of time to decay. In order to keep this time short so that the device can handle high frequencies it is beneficial to have the chips of silicon very small. On the other hand, in order to accommodate high currents and power levels the chips need to be relatively large. Small signal diodes can operate at high switching speeds, but can not handle high currents. Normal rectifiers can handle high currents, but will not operate efficiently at high speeds.

It would be untrue to say that a combination of high power and high speed operation is impossible using semiconductors, but even with significant advances over the years, such a combination remains problematic. With both diodes and transistors, high power operation at very high frequencies requires the use of quite expensive devices. Where very high power levels are involved, and particularly where high frequencies are also involved, it is not uncommon for vacuum tube devices to still be used in preference to semiconductor components.

Parameters

This is a list of the parameters you are likely to encounter in short-form data sheets for diodes, complete with a brief explanation of each one.

PIV

This is the "peak inverse voltage" (sometimes termed Vrrm). As its name suggests, this is the peak reverse bias voltage that should be applied to the device. Semiconductors tend to be quite voltage conscious, and even slightly exceeding this voltage rating for a very brief period of time could result in the device being damaged. Remember that the peak voltage in an a.c. signal is about 1.42 times its r.m.s. level.

If

The If rating is the maximum average current that should be allowed to flow with the component forward biased. As already mentioned, semiconductor devices are easily damaged by excessive voltages, but they are much more tolerant of high current pulses. A rectifier that can handle an average forward current of up to one amp may well be able to handle pulses of up to about ten times this figure, provided they are suitably brief. This is just as well, since in a mains power supply circuit it is brief pulses at a high current that flow through the rectifiers, as the smoothing capacitor is "topped-up" on the peak of each half cycle.

IR

This is the maximum reverse current that will flow with a given reverse bias voltage. This figure is normally quoted at a potential which is equal to or very close to the component's PIV rating. For silicon diodes it is usually a fraction of a microamp, but for germanium types it can be as high as a few hundred microamps.

VF drop

The VF drop figure is often quoted for rectifiers, and is the maximum voltage drop through the device when it is forward biased by a specified current. This current is usually the If rating of the component. Although silicon rectifiers start to conduct with a forward bias of only about 0.5 to 0.7 volts, and they conduct heavily thereafter, there is some increase in the voltage drop as the forward current is increased. With high currents being passed, this voltage increase can be quite significant. Most rectifiers have voltage drops of up to about 1.0 to 1.2 volts when operating at their maximum current rating. This drop obviously needs to be taken into account when designing power supply circuits.

Trr

This is the recovery time of the component, or the time it takes to switch off in other words. Fast recovery rectifiers generally have Trr times of around 30 to 40ns.

Rectifiers are available as modules containing four components in the bridge configuration. With these it is common for the maximum r.m.s. input voltage of the bridge circuit to be quoted, rather than the PIV of the individual diodes. The data for these components often quotes a maximum load capacitance, which is simply the maximum acceptable value for the smoothing capacitor into which the component feeds. Although the smoothing capacitance may not seem to be something that has a significant effect on the operating conditions of the rectifier, it does in fact have quite a significant effect. The higher the smoothing capacitance, the shorter but larger the pulses of current that "top-up" the smoothing capacitor.

Diodes and rectifiers have been manufactured using a variety of encapsulations, several of which are now obsolete,

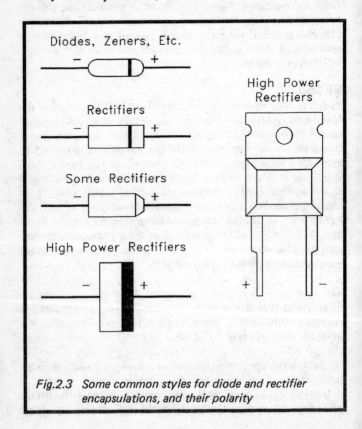

Fig.2.3   Some common styles for diode and rectifier encapsulations, and their polarity

and have been so for many years. Figure 2.3 shows most of the current encapsulations. As a diode is a polarised component it is essential that there is some method of indicating the component's polarity. For most diodes and rectifiers this takes the form of a coloured band around one end of the component. This band indicates the cathode ("+" or "k") end of the device. Some diodes, a little unhelpfully, have several coloured bands. These indicate the type number in a fashion which is reminiscent of resistor colour coding. You may encounter this system on the popular 1N4148 silicon signal diode, which has yellow − brown − yellow − grey as its four band marking. The bands are offset towards one end of the component, and this is the cathode end.

Bridge rectifiers generally have the input terminals or leads marked with "∼" signs, and the outputs marked "+" and "−", leaving no room for confusion.

Specials

There are a number of specialised types of diode, but some of these are so specialised that you are unlikely to ever encounter them. Here we will consider a few of the more common specialised types. We start with the Schottky diodes. The term "Schottky" is quite well known in electronics, but mainly as a description of a family of 74** series logic integrated circuits. A Schottky diode is a special type which is designed to have a much lower forward voltage drop than an ordinary silicon diode. In fact it has a forward voltage drop more like that of a germanium device. In low power Schottky integrated circuits, these diodes are used to prevent transistors from switching on to saturation point. This has the benefits of slightly reduced power consumption, and substantially improved operating speed. Schottky diodes are available as discrete components (such as the BAR28), but are admittedly something of a rarity. They can be used in any small signal application where fast switching speed and a low forward voltage drop are of benefit. At about ten times the cost of ordinary small signal diodes they are too expensive for general use.

Variable capacitance diodes, or "varicaps" as they are often called, are in essence just ordinary silicon diodes. A diode

61

such as a 1N4148 can in fact be used as a variable capacitance type, but its capacitance range will be something of an unknown quantity, making it impossible to obtain predictable results. A proper varicap has a capacitance swing that is guaranteed to be within certain quite stringent limits.

A varicap utilizes the fact that as the reverse bias fed to a P — N junction is increased, the depletion layer becomes wider. In effect, the pieces of P type and N type semiconductor material are the plates of the capacitor, and the depletion layer is the dielectric. Increasing the reverse bias increases the effective width of the dielectric, and gives reduced capacitance. For ordinary diodes the capacitance swing obtained is not very great, being typically something like 5p to 25p for a 0 to 30 volt input. This is adequate for applications such as v.h.f. receivers, and short wave communications equipment that covers only small bands of frequencies. It is inadequate for something like a medium and long wave radio set, where a capacitance swing of about 20p to 200p or more is required. However, special devices designed specifically for operation in medium and long wave broadcast sets are produced, and these can provide capacitance swings of around 25p to 400p from a 0 to 15 volt tuning voltage.

An obvious problem with varicaps is that they provide a diode action as well as providing a variable capacitance. The diode action may be irrelevant in some cases, but in others it could result in unacceptable distortions to the processed signal. The standard method of reducing problems with unwanted rectification of processed signals is the one shown in Figure 2.4. The advantage of this back-to-back arrangement is that it gives no path of conduction through both diodes with an input signal of either polarity. Its drawbacks are that two diodes are required, and that the capacitance swing obtained is only half that of a single diode.

Zener Diodes
Zener diodes are used in voltage stabiliser circuits. With the advent of high quality monolithic voltage regulators that cost surprisingly little in most cases, they are perhaps used less at present than they were a few years ago. They still represent an important diode sub-category though, and are used in a fair

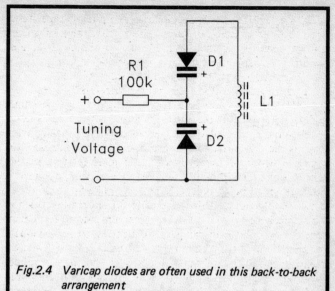

Fig.2.4   Varicap diodes are often used in this back-to-back arrangement

percentage of circuits.

Like varicaps, zeners are basically just ordinary silicon diodes. Any silicon diode that is subjected to a steadily increasing reverse bias will eventually breakdown and pass a very high current. The decrease in resistance is very pronounced indeed, with a reverse resistance of typically many tens of megohms or more suddenly being reduced to a few tens of ohms or less. The voltage at which this breakdown occurs is termed the "avalanche" voltage.

Obviously there is the potential for the diode to be destroyed when the avalanche voltage is exceeded. In a practical voltage stabiliser circuit a load resistor is placed in series with the zener, as in Figure 2.5, and it limits the current flow to a safe level so that the device can operate safely. A capacitor is normally placed in parallel with the zener diode, as in the circuit of Figure 2.5, to suppress the noise spikes that tend to be generated by the zener diode. Although a zener diode has a well defined avalanche voltage, it is not so well

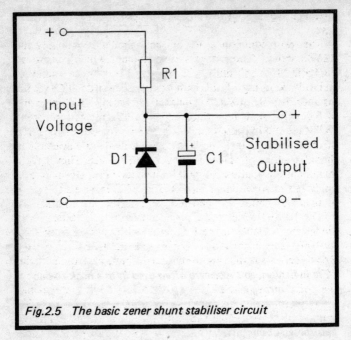

Input
Voltage

R1

D1

C1

Stabilised
Output

+

−

+

−

Fig.2.5 The basic zener shunt stabiliser circuit

defined that it genuinely triggers straight from a very high
resistance to virtually zero resistance. Consequently, the
regulation provided is something less than perfect. For components having voltage ratings of about 6.8 volts or more the
efficiency is quite good though, and is adequate for most
purposes. Lower voltage zener diodes tend to be much less
efficient, and will often permit quite significant variations in
the output voltage unless they are fed with a reasonably
constant current.

At one time there were several ranges of zener diode
available, including quite high power and high voltage types.
Basic zener shunt stabilisers are little used in high power
circuits these days since they are rather inefficient, and tend
to generate a lot of heat. A series regulator using a low power
zener stabiliser circuit (or some other voltage reference) is
generally a more satisfactory method. For high output
voltages an active voltage regulator based on a low voltage

reference voltage generator is the usual type used these days.

The most common series of zener diodes is probably the BZY88 series. These have a type number which consists of the basic "BZY88" plus "C", meaning ±5% voltage tolerance, and voltage rating of the component. The BZY88C8V2 for instance, is a BZY88 series zener diode having a voltage rating of 8.2 volts. As is now the accepted norm in electronics, the "V" is used to indicate that the units are volts, and the position of the decimal point. The BZY88 zener diodes are available in the E24 series of values from 2.7 to 33 volts. They have a maximum dissipation of 400 milliwatts (also given as 500 milliwatts in some data sources). The voltages have a tolerance of plus and minus 5%, and are for a current of 5 milliamps.

The BZX61 series has a power rating of 1.3 watts. These diodes are available in the E24 series, with voltages from 4.7V to 100V and a tolerance of plus and minus 5%. Like the BZY88 series, the full type number is the basic part number, plus "C", indicating the voltage tolerance, and the voltage rating of the component (e.g. BZX61C10V for a 10 volt component).

As pointed out previously, zener diodes produce a certain amount of noise. While this is normally a nuisance and has to be suppressed by a smoothing capacitor, it also permits zener diodes to be used as the basis of noise generators. They produce a significant output over a wide frequency range. There are special noise diodes which are guaranteed to produce good quality white noise when used under the specified operating conditions. These are usually only intended to be used over the audio frequency range. These diodes would seem to be difficult to obtain these days.

Tunnel diodes are one of the more interesting forms of diode, but seem to be very difficult to obtain these days. They have an unusual forward transfer characteristic that initially provides what is virtually pure resistance. Increasing the input voltage further causes the current flow to decrease, and having dropped to virtually zero, it then starts to increase again. This may not seem particularly spectacular, but things are perhaps more interesting if the process is considered in reverse. As the bias voltage is reduced, the current flow decreases, then increases, and finally decreases again. The important point to note is that over part of the transfer characteristic there is effectively negative resistance, with a decrease in the applied voltage giving increased current flow. This effect is not normally used to provide amplification, and the normal role of tunnel diodes are as oscillators. They are used in a form of relaxation oscillator. They are mainly used in v.h.f. and u.h.f. equipment, and will operate quite happily at frequencies of several hundred megahertz.

Transistors

Transistors are slightly more complex devices than diodes, as they consist of three pieces of semiconductor material. This can either be a piece of N type material sandwiched between two slices of P type material (a pnp transistor), or a piece of P type material sandwiched between two slices of N type semiconductor (an npn transistor). Germanium transistors can be (and often are) made using a technique that is similar to the one used for germanium diodes. It differs from the diode method in that both sides of the N type substrate are processed, so as to give the required npn structure.

Silicon transistors are produced using what is an extended and more refined version of the technique used to manufacture silicon diodes. It requires the use of photo-resists and masks, and produces "planar" transistors. Planar simply means flat, which is a pretty fair description of the semiconductor structure produced by this manufacturing process. It is quite a complex process, but Figure 2.6 shows the basic way in which transistors are formed on the silicon wafer. First a large and deep area of the substrate is processed so as to produce a large piece of P type semiconductor. Then further processing is carried out to turn some of the P type material back to N type semiconductor. This gives the required npn structure, and although the form of the device is not with three nice neat slices of semiconductor material, it will work perfectly well. It has to be stressed that this description of things is highly over-simplified, and that it actually takes numerous stages to get to the point where the wafer is ready to be diced up and the individual transistors can be cased and connected up to leadout wires.

A transistor is a three terminal device, with a leadout wire

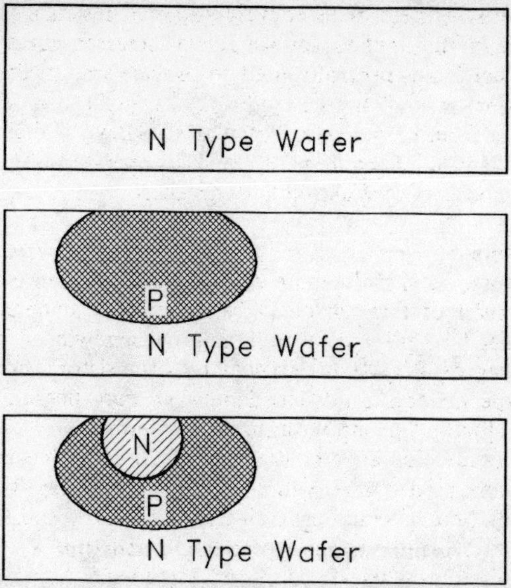

Fig.2.6 Processing a silicon wafer can produce this planar npn structure

being connected to each piece of semiconductor material. The three terminals are called the "emitter", "base", and "collector". Figure 2.7 shows which terminal connects to each piece of semiconductor material. Although a transistor might seem to be more or less symmetrical, it will not operate properly if the connections to the emitter and collector terminals are reversed. The structure is not truly symmetrical in that the pieces of semiconductor material are of different sizes. If used with the emitter and collector terminals reversed, a silicon transistor will often operate, but in a rather limited and inefficient manner. If a germanium transistor is used in

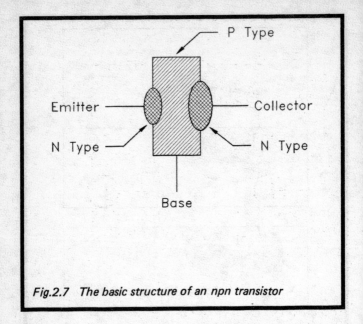

Fig.2.7 The basic structure of an npn transistor

this manner the most likely result is that it will be destroyed!

The basic action of a transistor is to provide current gain. The circuits of Figure 2.8 show basic transistor test setups. These are for npn transistors (Fig. 2.8(a)) and pnp transistors (Fig. 2.8(b)). These are essentially the same, and only differ in that the supply potentials are different. An npn transistor is normally operated with its collector and base terminals positive of the emitter, while pnp devices are normally operated with these terminals negative with respect to the emitter.

VR1 provides a variable base current, while ME1 registers the collector current. With no base current applied to the test component there should be no significant collector current. The npn or pnp structure gives what are effectively two back-to-back diodes, and whichever polarity the supply has, one junction will always block a significant current flow. In practice a small current will flow, and this is called the "leakage" current. For a silicon device this current is usually very small,

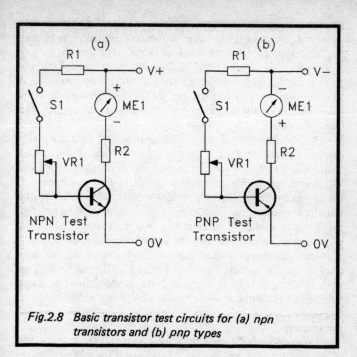

Fig.2.8 Basic transistor test circuits for (a) npn transistors and (b) pnp types

at under one microamp. In fact it is only a very small fraction of a microamp in most cases. It is generally much higher for germanium transistors — possibly a milliamp or more. Circuits which use germanium transistors have to be designed in such a way that they can cope with large variations in the leakage currents of these components. Their high leakage currents is probably one of the factors that has led to germanium transistors declining to the point where they are virtually all obsolete.

If we ignore leakage currents, which are insignificant anyway with practically all modern transistors, the collector current is controlled by the base current. If the base current is steadily increased, the collector current will increase as well. The point to note here is that the collector current will always be much larger than the base current. If the base current is one microamp, the collector current might be one hundred microamps. If the base current is increased to

2 microamps, the collector current will then increase to two hundred microamps. In other words, the transistor is providing a current gain of one hundred times. The current gain of a transistor is equal to the collector current divided by the base current. This assumes an insignificant leakage current. If the leakage level is quite high, the leakage current must be deducted from the collector current before dividing it by the base current.

This explanation of the function provided by a transistor is somewhat idealised. In reality, no transistor provides perfect linearity. In fact no amplifying devices are at present capable of providing completely distortion-free amplification. If our example transistor provides a collector current of one hundred microamps from a base current of one microamp, with the base current increased to two microamps the collector current would probably be something like two hundred and ten microamps. The gain of most transistors increases slightly as the collector current is raised. This only occurs up to a point, and at high collector currents the gain often starts to fall away slightly.

Parameters
The semiconductor section of component catalogues often seem to contain a lot of data. This is very useful to the more experienced electronics hobbyist, but can be a little confusing for newcomers to the hobby. Most of the parameters you are likely to encounter are fairly straightforward though. This list of important parameters plus explanatory notes should help to clarify the exact meaning of most of the transistor parameters you are likely to encounter.

HFE
This is the d.c. current gain, and should be specified at a particular collector to emitter voltage and collector current. As pointed out previously, the gain of a transistor varies significantly with changes in collector current, and an HFE figure is virtually meaningless unless a collector current is quoted. There is far less variation in gain with changes in collector to emitter voltage, provided this voltage is not extremely low. The absence of a specified collector voltage

70

for the HFE figure is therefore a much less serious omission. The current gains quoted in brief data are usually maximum and minimum figures, and for many devices a wide range of gain levels are acceptable. Something like a gain of between 125 and 900 would not be untypical. Sometimes an "average" or "typical" figure is quoted, and it then needs to be borne in mind that the actual gain of any given device of that type might be well removed from the quoted figure.

Hfe

This parameter differs from HFE in that it is not the gain at d.c., but with a small a.c. signal.

VCBO

This is the highest voltage that should be connected across the collector and base terminals with the emitter left open circuit (i.e. with the emitter left unconnected). Exceeding this voltage is likely to result in the component breaking down, and the result of this would almost certainly be to render it unusable.

VCEO

The VCEO rating is similar to the VCBO type, but it is the maximum voltage that should be applied across the collector and emitter terminals with the base left open circuit. This voltage rating is usually somewhat less than the VCBO rating, and is consequently the one that in most applications will determine the maximum usable supply voltage for the device in question.

Tj

Tj is the junction temperature rating of the component. In other words, it is the maximum temperature to which the semiconductor material should be subjected. Exceeding this rating is very likely to result in serious damage to the device, and in extreme cases overheated semiconductors can explode with a loud "crack"! Even using a component just below its Tj rating will probably significantly reduce its reliability. It is important to realise that this rating is the maximum tempera-ture to which the chip of semiconductor material should be allowed to rise. There will not be perfect thermal contact between the chip and the outside of its encapsulation. Consequently, the case temperature must always be well below the Tj rating in order to ensure that the chip also remains comfortably below the relevant temperature. For germanium transistors the Tj figure is often quite low, but for silicon devices it can be (and often is) as high as 175 to 200 degrees Centigrade. Be warned that many power devices run at temperatures that can lead to burnt fingers if you should touch them.

Ptot

This is the maximum power rating of the device. As the base current is almost invariably very low in comparison to the collector current, for practical purposes the power dissipated by a transistor can be obtained by multiplying the collector to emitter voltage by the collector current. When dealing with Ptot ratings you need to keep in mind that they are the maximum power rating under given sets of operating conditions. For a small signal device, the only operating condition specified might be the ambient temperature, which would normally be 25 degrees Centigrade. Running a transistor at its Ptot rating would then be acceptable, provided the ambient temperature would never be more than 25 degrees Centigrade. In practice this could probably not be guaranteed, and the power level would have to be kept substantially below the Ptot rating. For power transistors the Ptot rating is often given under the assumption that the device is mounted on a very large heatsink, or even a notional infinite heatsink. A heatsink, incidentally, is merely a piece of metal (usually finned) that is used to conduct heat away from the transistor and into the surrounding air. Under practical operating conditions the Ptot power rating may not be usable. Without a heatsink, even 10% of the Ptot figure could be sufficient to cause a power device to overheat.

When dealing with Ptot ratings remember that you must keep devices within their area of safe operation. In other words, there are often collector voltage and current combinations that give acceptable power ratings, but which will produce local "hot spots" in the semiconductor structure, causing

the device to breakdown and be destroyed. The manufacturers' full data should include a graph showing the area of
safe operation.

VEBO

When forward biased, the base – emitter terminals of a transistor behave very much like a forward biased diode junction.
No significant current flows until the forward threshold
voltage of about 0.6 volts is exceeded, after which quite a
modest increase in voltage will cause a large current to flow.
The base – emitter junction also operates very much like an
ordinary diode if it is reverse biased. No significant current
flows until the breakdown voltage is reached, and then the
device avalanches. This breakdown voltage is quite low for
most transistors, with somewhere between 5 and 8 volts being
the norm. Like a reverse biased diode or zener diode, exceeding the breakdown voltage will not result in any damage to the
device provided the current flow is limited to a safe level. The
VEBO is the reverse breakdown voltage rating of the transistor.
It is measured with the collector left open circuit, but connecting the collector into circuit will not usually have any any
significant affect on this rating. Although this rating might
seem of only academic importance, it should be kept in mind
that where capacitive coupling is used into the base of a
transistor, it can be reverse biased by strong signals of the
appropriate type. This is not likely to occur in applications
such as audio amplification, but it can easily occur in oscillator circuits. Due to the relatively low breakdown voltage,
this can result in some oscillator circuits not operating in the
expected manner.

IC

The IC rating is the maximum collector current that the component can safely handle. This is normally quoted in the form
of the maximum continuous current that can be safely accom-
modated. However, for some medium power devices intended
for switching applications it is a figure for pulsed operation
that is quoted.

fT

This is the transition frequency, which is merely the frequency at which the current gain of the device falls to unity. This is normally quoted for the device when it is operated in the common emitter amplifying mode. This is an important parameter, as it obviously gives a clear indication of the maximum frequency at which the device is likely to provide a useful amount of amplification. Apart from indicating the frequency at which the current gain falls to unity, it also shows the maximum gain that can be achieved at lower frequencies. The maximum gain possible at lower frequencies is equal to the transition frequency divided by the frequency at which a gain figure is required. A device having an fT of 300MHz for instance, would have a gain of 30 at 10MHz (300MHz divided by 10MHz equals 30). This is an over simplification in that it assumes that the transistor has infinite current gain. The gain at low frequencies is obviously limited by the HFE figure of the component.

ICBO

This is merely the leakage current of the transistor. In other words, it is the current that flows between the collector and emitter terminals with the base terminal left open circuit. This parameter is very temperature dependent, but for a silicon device it is normally under one microamp and totally insignificant. It can be quite high for germanium transistors, especially certain power types (although these are now long obsolete).

VCEsat

The VCEsat parameter is more usually just referred to as the saturation voltage. If a strong base current is applied to a transistor that is connected to operate as a simple common emitter switching stage, it will switch on and provide a very low output voltage. The VCEsat rating is a notional minimum collector voltage that can be achieved with the device in this simple switching mode. In reality it is not the lowest collector voltage that can be achieved. If a steadily increasing forward bias is applied to a common emitter switch, the collector voltage will rapidly fall to a low level, and thereafter it will reduce very gradually. The saturation voltage is one into the part of the transfer characteristic where collector voltage has "bottomed out", but it is not usually the absolute minimum collector voltage that can be achieved.

tON

When a base current is applied to a transistor it takes a certain amount of time for the device to respond to it and switch on. This is the time specified in the tON parameter. Like VCEsat, this is a parameter that is mostly only of importance in logic and other switching applications.

tOFF

This is similar to tON, but it is the time taken for the transistor to switch off once its base current has been removed. Due to storage effects, the tOFF time for a transistor that has been biased into saturation is much longer than the tON time.

Unijunctions

Unijunction transistors (u.j.t.s) were all the rage about fifteen to twenty-five years ago, but seem to be little used these days. They have been superseded by timer integrated circuits and other devices. These transistors have little in common with ordinary types, can not be used as amplifiers, and it is debatable as to whether or not they should really be called transistors at all. The term "transistor" is supposedly a contraction of "transfer resistor", which refers to the ability of a transistor to vary its collector to emitter resistance in response to a changing input current. A unijunction transistor does not really provide what could reasonably be regarded as a comparable function.

The unijunction name is derived from the fact that a transistor of this type has just one junction, and not the two of a standard bipolar device. It has two base terminals (base 1 and base 2), and an emitter terminal, but no collector. In use a unijunction transistor is invariably connected in the relaxation oscillator configuration of Figure 2.9, although in some cases it is in somewhat disguised form. Between the two base terminals there is a bar of silicon semiconductor material, and this provides a resistance of typically about 3k to 10k.

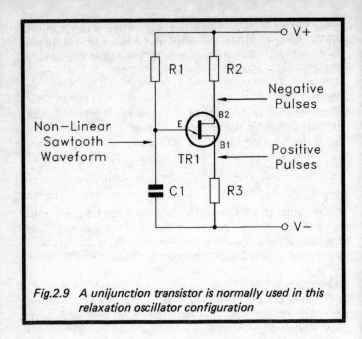

Fig.2.9 A unijunction transistor is normally used in this relaxation oscillator configuration

Somewhere towards the middle of the bar, but usually offset towards the base 2 terminal, there is a p-n junction.

On the face of it, the circuit will do nothing particularly spectacular. There will be a current flow of a few milliamps through R2, the base 1 to base 2 resistance of the transistor, and R3. C1 will initially charge up via R1, but the diode formed by the p-n junction will become forward biased when the potential on C1 reaches something in the region of 70% of the supply voltage. Although one might expect the current flow through R1 to then be diverted into the emitter circuit of the transistor, with nothing further happening, matters are a bit more complex than this in practice. Due to a regenerative action within the transistor, when the potential on C1 reaches this point the unijunction "fires". Its emitter to base 1 resistance then falls to a very low level, resulting in C1 rapidly discharging through this route and via R3. This continues until the charge on C1 drops to a very low level,

76

whereupon the unijunction transistor reverts to its original state. C1 then starts to charge up via R1, with the unijunction "firing" again when the appropriate charge voltage is reached. This process continues indefinitely, with the circuit acting as a simple relaxation oscillator. This gives short positive pulses from the base 1 terminal, brief negative pulses from the base 2 terminal, and a non-linear sawtooth waveform at the emitter terminal.

Parameters

As one would expect, the parameters in data sheets for unijunction transistors are totally different to those for ordinary bipolar types. This is a list and brief explanation of the main ones.

VBB

The maximum permissible base 1 to base 2 voltage.

IP

This is the peak point current, which is the minimum emitter current needed to trigger the device. If the timing resistor value in a unijunction relaxation oscillator is made too high, this current will not be reached and oscillation will not occur.

IV

IV is the valley point current, or the minimum current needed to hold the device in the triggered state in other words.

IE

The maximum emitter current rating. This is a peak rating, not a continuous one.

PTOT

The maximum dissipation for the device.

RBB

The base 1 to base 2 resistance.

n

This is the intrinsic stand-off ratio. In effect, it is a measure of where on the silicon bar the p-n junction is placed. With it three-quarters of the way up from the base 1 terminal for instance, the intrinsic stand-off ratio would be 0.75.

77

FETs

Unlike unijunction transistors, the various field effect transistors (f.e.t.s) seem to have become more popular over the years. There seem to be more devices and more varieties of f.e.t. available than ever before. The original type of f.e.t. is the junction gate f.e.t., or just "Jfet" as they are popularly known. These were later joined by various types of MOSFET (metal oxide silicon field effect transistors). These devices can be used in amplifying modes that are broadly similar to those used for bipolar transistors. The terminals have different names though, and there are some radical differences between bipolar and f.e.t. devices. The base, emitter, and collector of a bipolar transistor are equivalent to the gate, source, and drain terminals of a f.e.t.

An essential difference between bipolar and field effect transistors is that whereas bipolar devices are current operated, field effect devices are voltage operated. In other words, it is the voltage applied to the gate of a field effect transistor that is of importance, not the gate current. The input resistances of field effect transistors are so high that the gate currents are extremely low indeed. The input resistance of a Jfet is usually in excess of one thousand megohms, while that of a MOSFET can often exceed one million megohms! While the input impedance at low frequencies is similarly high, it reduces substantially at medium and high frequencies due to the input capacitance. This is typically about 10p, but in the common source amplifying mode this is effectively multiplied by the gain of the device due to the Miller Effect.

Jfets and some MOSFETs are depletion mode devices. With a bipolar transistor the device is normally switched off, and it is turned on by applying a forward bias. A depletion mode field effect device is switched on quite hard with zero gate bias, and in normal operation it is given a reverse bias so that it can provide reasonably linear operation. This reverse bias is normally provided via a resistor in the source circuit, plus another resistor to bias the gate to the 0 volt supply rail. This is very much like the bias circuits used in valve circuits, and in some respects field effect transistors are more like valves than bipolar devices.

Jfets are widely used in both audio and radio frequency

78

circuits, but are perhaps somewhat rarer in audio circuits than they once were. They seem to have been largely ousted in this role by integrated circuits, including operational amplifiers having low noise Jfet input stages. MOSFETs are little used in audio frequency equipment, but appear in many pieces of radio frequency equipment. In particular, they are much used in the r.f. and mixer stages of high frequency (h.f.), very high frequency (v.h.f.), and ultra high frequency (u.h.f.) radio receiving equipment. Good MOSFET r.f. and mixer stages can provide excellent large signal handling and noise performance.

Dual gate MOSFETs are often used for mixer stages. As their name implies, they have two gate terminals. Although one might reasonably expect that this would result in the output simply responding to the sum of the two input voltages, it does not work this way in practice. The gain from one gate to the output is controlled by the voltage at the other gate. In a radio receiver mixer stage application, feeding the input signal to one gate and the oscillator signal to the other gate therefore gives the required complex mixing action needed to provide the heterodyne effect. If a dual gate MOSFET is utilized in an r.f. stage, the input signal can be applied to one gate, with the other gate being given either a fixed bias level or being fed with a variable bias from the automatic gain control (a.g.c.) circuit.

The MOSFETs that are generally available seem to be depletion mode devices. There are such things as "enhancement" mode MOSFETs, which are more like bipolar devices than the standard depletion mode devices. They are normally switched off, and require a forward bias to bring them into conduction. Being field effect devices, it is still the input voltage rather than the gate current that is of importance. It is transistors of this type that are used in CMOS logic integrated circuits incidentally.

I suppose that power field effect transistors still tend to be regarded as something new, and it is true that they are relatively new in comparison to Jfets and MOSFETs. However, they have been generally available for what must be almost ten years now. There are two main types available, which are the VMOS and power MOSFET varieties. The

VMOS transistors derive their name from their "V" shaped structure. Whereas ordinary field effect transistors have "on" resistances of about 100 to 500 ohms, the structure of VMOS transistors enables them to produce drain to source resistances of 2 ohms or less. This permits them to control quite high currents. Some devices are capable of controlling currents of several amps. Power MOSFETs have a different structure, but have broadly similar characteristics to VMOS devices.

Both types of power f.e.t. tend to be significantly more expensive than good quality bipolar power transistors capable of handling comparable power levels. Also, they are probably more easily damaged than bipolar power transistors. They do have a few distinct advantages though. Perhaps the most obvious one is the enormous power gain they provide. A swing of a few volts at a negligible current can control output powers of as much as a hundred watts, or even more. Switching speeds are very fast for power devices. Thermal stability is another factor in their favour. As mentioned previously in this chapter, bipolar devices have to be operated in their so-called area of safe operation. Certain combinations of collector current and voltage cause what is termed "secondary breakdown", which results in local "hot spots" in the semiconductor structure, and the destruction of the device. With virtually all power f.e.t.s, source voltage and current combinations that provide acceptable power dissipation figures are acceptable.

In a similar vein, linear power amplifiers that use bipolar power transistors often have to combat thermal runaway. This is where heating in the output transistors causes them to draw a heavier current, which in turn results in the output transistors heating up further, which results in a still higher current being drawn, and so on. If left unchecked this leads to the output transistors eventually overheating and being destroyed. This problem does not occur with power f.e.t.s as at medium and high currents they have a slightly negative temperature coefficient. In other words, rather than heating of these devices causing a higher current to flow, it results in a very slightly reduced current consumption. This makes the quiescent current consumption quite stable, and totally rules

80

out any risk of thermal runaway.

Parameters

Obviously field effect transistors are very different to bipolar transistors in many respects, and accordingly they have a largely different set of parameters. This is a list of the main parameters, together with a brief explanation of each one.

fT

This is basically the same as the fT rating of a bipolar device, but it is, of course, the unity gain bandwidth in the common source amplifying mode (the equivalent of the bipolar common emitter mode).

PT

PT is an exact equivalent to PTOT for a bipolar transistor (i.e. the maximum permissible power rating).

Vp

Vp is the pinch-off voltage. This is the reverse gate to source voltage needed to switch off a depletion mode field effect transistor. Obviously this parameter is not applicable to enhancement mode devices.

VGS

This is the maximum permissible gate to source voltage, and is roughly analogous to VCBO for a bipolar transistor. However, no avalanche effect is obtained with field effect devices. Note that some power f.e.t.s (particularly the VMOS variety) are protected by a zener diode against excessive gate voltages.

VDG

VDG is the maximum permissible drain to gate voltage, and is roughly equivalent to VCBO for a bipolar transistor.

VDS

The maximum drain to source voltage, and the f.e.t. equivalent of VCEO.

Ciss

This is the input capacitance with the component used in the common source amplifying mode.

gm

The gm rating is the small signal common source transconductance. As the f.e.t. method of gain measurement, this is roughly equivalent to HFE for a bipolar transistor, but is only a rough equivalent. Remember that with a field effect transistor we are not dealing in terms of input and output current, but with input voltage and output current. This parameter is therefore a measurement of how much the output current changes with a given variation in the gate voltage. Conductance is similar to resistance, but is essentially the inverse of it. It is a measure of how well something conducts electricity instead of a measurement of how much it resists a current flow. The unit of measurement used for conductance and transconductance is the "mho" or "siemens". The gm formula of current divided by voltage is the inverse of that used to calculate resistance using Ohm's Law, and the term "mho" is supposedly derived from this, and is simply "ohm" spelled backwards! If a f.e.t. had a transconductance rating of 12 mmhos (12 millimhos, or twelve thousandths of a mho), a change in the gate voltage of one volt would result in the drain current changing by 12 milliamps.

VGS(th)

This is the gate threshold voltage, and it only applies to enhancement mode devices. It is the forward bias voltage at which the device begins to switch on. This is similar to the 0.6 volts or thereabouts needed before a silicon bipolar transistor will start to turn on, but for enhancement mode f.e.t.s the turn on threshold voltage is generally about one to two volts.

IDSS

IDSS is the enhancement mode f.e.t. equivalent to leakage (ICBO) in a bipolar transistor. It is the drain current that flows with zero gate bias voltage. Even for power f.e.t. devices this figure is normally quite low (a few microamps or less), and it is not normally of any significance in practice.

IGSS

This parameter is the gate body leakage current. It is merely the gate current that flows for a given gate voltage. Due to the very high input resistance of f.e.t.s this rating is normally no more than a nanoamp or two, but it can be a few microamps for power f.e.t.s under worst case conditions.

ID

This parameter is normally only specified for power f.e.t.s, and it is the maximum permissible drain current.

IDss

This is the drain current that flows through a depletion mode f.e.t. that is subjected to zero gate to source voltage. Using this figure and the gm parameter it is possible to calculate the drain current for other gate bias levels. However, the tolerances on both gm and IDss ratings are often quite high. The tolerance on the IDss parameter in particular is usually quite large, with the maximum figure being perhaps as much as ten times higher than the minimum one. This makes accurate biasing of many depletion mode f.e.t.s a difficult task.

ton

This is simply the switch on time for the device.

toff

The toff rating is the switch off time for the device. Unlike bipolar switch on/off time ratings, the turn on and turn off delays for f.e.t.s are often the same.

RDS

This is simply the drain to source resistance with the device fully switched on.

VDS(on)

This could reasonably be regarded as the power f.e.t. equivalent to saturation voltage. It is the drain to source voltage with the device heavily forward biased and conducting a specified current.

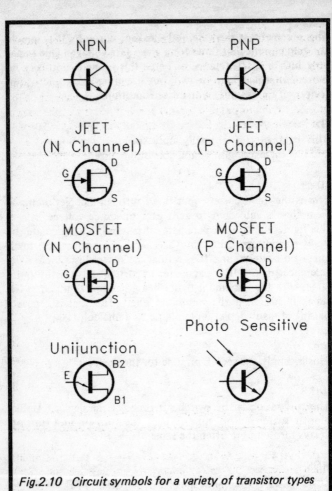

Fig.2.10 *Circuit symbols for a variety of transistor types*

Figure 2.10 shows the circuit symbols for a variety of transistors, including f.e.t. types. Note that there are slight variations in transistor circuit symbols, and the f.e.t. types in particular vary slightly from one publication to another.

SCRs

Silicon controlled rectifiers (s.c.r.s) are a form of semiconductor switching device. They can provide massive power gains, with minute input signals controlling output powers of up to a few hundred watts, or even more with some high power devices. They are strictly on/off switching devices though, and are totally unsuitable for any form of linear amplification. The basic type of s.c.r. is more commonly called a "thyristor".

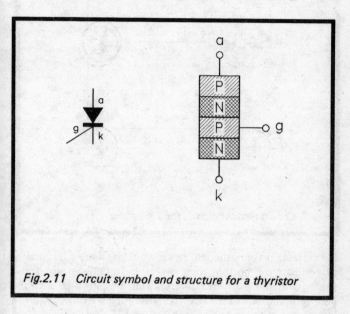

Fig.2.11   Circuit symbol and structure for a thyristor

A thyristor is a four layer device. It has three terminals which are called the gate, anode, and cathode. Figure 2.11 shows the circuit symbol and basic construction for a device of this type. On the face of it, we have what is just two P–N diode junctions connected in series, giving a diode action with double the normal voltage drop through the component. A closer examination reveals that the middle two layers also form a diode junction, but having an opposite polarity to the other two. Consequently, the device will not actually conduct in either direction. The addition of the gate terminal

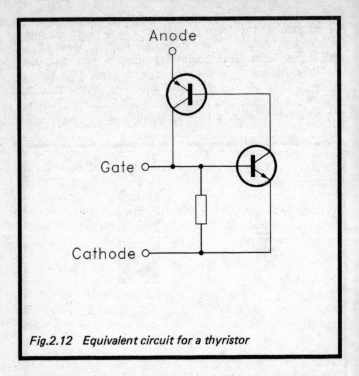

Fig.2.12 Equivalent circuit for a thyristor

complicates matters though, and it would be more appropriate to consider the bottom three layers as forming an npn transistor, with the top three layers forming a pnp type with its base terminal not externally accessible. This gives an equivalent circuit of the type shown in Figure 2.12.

Normally both transistors are switched off, and the device will not conduct between its anode and cathode terminals. Giving a positive bias current to the gate terminal results in the npn transistor starting to switch on. It then provides a base current to the pnp device, which in turn provides the npn transistor with an increased base current. This gives a regenerative action which ends with both transistors biased hard into conduction. The component then conducts between its anode and cathode terminals, provided the anode is the more positive of the two. There is a voltage drop of about 1.2 volts or so through the component.

Unlike transistors, thyristors do not switch off once the input current is removed. If this is done, the two transistors keep each other switched on, and the removal of the input current has no noticeable effect at all. This is not to say that once switched on, a thyristor will remain that way for ever! Reducing the current flow through the device to a low level (typically about 10 to 20 milliamps) will cause it to switch off. If the device is handling a pulsing signal of some kind (such as the rectified mains supply), it will switch off towards the end of each input pulse. In effect, it will then only remain switched on for as long as the gate bias is applied. If a non-pulsing signal is being controlled, the device must be switched off by either momentarily breaking the circuit, or diverting the current away from the thyristor. For applications of this type it is usually much easier to use a switching transistor rather than a thyristor.

Parameters

There are a number of important thyristor parameters to be found in data on these devices. A list of the main parameters, together with a short explanation of each one, is provided below.

Vr

This is the maximum reverse voltage rating of the device (i.e. the maximum voltage with the anode taken negative of the cathode). This is usually a peak voltage, whereas a.c. voltages are generally given as r.m.s. figures. The peak voltage is equivalent to about 1.42 times the r.m.s. level (e.g. about 340 volts for the 240 volt U.K. mains supply).

Vf

This is the maximum forward voltage rating (i.e. the maximum voltage with the anode taken positive of the cathode).

If

If is the maximum forward current that the device can handle. It is either an average or r.m.s. figure, and the peak level can safely be very much higher than this.

Vg

The Vg rating is the maximum gate voltage that will be needed in order to trigger the component. This is typically about 1 volt or so.

Ig

This is the maximum gate current required to trigger the component. For older and higher power devices this figure can be quite high, at about 10 to 30 milliamps. For many recent thyristors it is much lower than this, at typically only about 200 microamps.

Ihm

Ihm is the maximum holding current. In other words, this is the minimum current that must be kept passing through the device in order to prevent it from switching off. It is not the current required in order to guarantee that the device will switch off (which is likely to be very much lower than the Ihm figure).

Vfm

As pointed out previosuly, there is a voltage drop through a thyristor that is about 1.2 volts or so. Vfm is the maximum forward voltage drop with the device operating at maximum current.

Triacs and Diacs

Triacs and diacs, which have the circuit symbols shown in Figure 2.13, are a development of the basic s.c.r. In fact a diac could be regarded as a step backwards, as it is a simple two terminal device. It is effectively a thyristor that has no gate terminal. Although this may seem a bit useless, with no way of triggering the device, this is not the case. If the forward voltage across the anode and cathode of a thyristor is made large enough, the device will break down and it will effectively trigger itself into conduction. A diac is designed to have quite a low breakdown voltage of typically about 30 to 35 volts (but much lower on some recent types). The main use of a diac is to trigger a thyristor or triac when the gate voltage reaches a certain level. This method is much used in

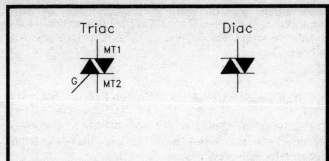

Fig.2.13   Triac and diac circuit symbols

lamp dimmers and other a.c. power control applications. Note
that a diac is bidirectional, and will operate with an input
voltage of either polarity.

A triac has similar characteristics to a thyristor, but it is
fully bidirectional.   It can be triggered by a gate signal of
either polarity, and can control a signal of either polarity.
A triac can therefore be used to control an a.c. load. This is
in fact possible with a thyristor, but only with the aid of a
rectifier circuit to ensure that it is fed with signals of the
appropriate polarity.

Type Numbers

Although you could easily get the impression that transistor
and diode type numbers are merely thought up at random by
the component manufacturers, there is usually some "rhyme
and reason" behind them. The amount of information contained in type numbers is strictly limited, and being realistic
about it, there is no way large amounts of data about a device
could be contained in a short type number. Type numbers
often provide a small but useful amount of information
though.

Many of the transistors and diodes used by U.K. hobbyists
have European Pro Electron type numbers. This method of
coding gives some basic information about the type of device
concerned. The first letter indicates the material used as the
basis of the device, and there are four letters currently in use.

89

These letters, plus the materials they represent, are listed below.

A   Germanium
B   Silicon
C   Gallium Arsenide
R   Compound Materials

The second letter indicates the general type of the device (rectifier, power transistor, etc.). This is a list of the letters and corresponding device types.

A   Small signal diode
B   Rectifier or variable capacitance diode
C   Small signal audio transistor
D   Power Transistor
E   Point contact diode
F   Low power high frequency transistor
G   Diode (oscillator, miscellaneous)
H   Diode (magnetic sensitive)
K   Hall Effect device (open magnetic circuit)
L   High frequency power transistor
M   Hall Effect device (closed magnetic circuit)
N   Opto-Isolator
P   Diode (radiation sensitive)
Q   Diode (radiation producing)
R   Special purpose device
S   Switching device (transistor or diode)
T   S.C.R. or triac
U   High voltage transistor
X   Rectifier or variable capacitance diode
Y   Power rectifier
Z   Zener diode

Devices that have this method of coding include many popular transistors, such as the popular BC series, which are clearly silicon small signal audio types. Some components which have this method of coding have a third letter (e.g. BFY51) which indicates that the device has been designed for the more demanding industrial applications, but does not really seem to be of any great significance. The number which follows the letters would seem to be a serial number, and it therefore gives an indication of how old or recent in design the component happens to be. Note though, that some devices with quite high numbers are the same as older components, but have a different encapsulation.

Gain Groups

A few transistors, and mainly the silicon lower power audio types, have a letter at the end of the type number. This indicates the gain grouping of the device. The current gain parameter of many transistors is pretty vague, with minimum and maximum figures of perhaps 125 and 900. Such wide tolerances can make it difficult to design circuits that will give predictable and repeatable results with any given device of that type. To minimise these problems some transistors are available in three gain groups, as well as the standard (ungrouped) version. This applies mainly to devices in the BC107/8/9 and BC177/8/9 series, and the gain-grouped devices have an "A", "B", or "C" suffix. These indicate the following generally accepted gain ranges.

A	110 to 220
B	200 to 450
C	420 to 800

Some transistors which have 2N series type numbers are also gain-grouped. Probably the best known example is the 2N2926, which was extremely popular at one time. The gain groupings for these devices are indicated by coloured spots, as detailed in this list.

Red	55 to 100
Orange	90 to 180
Yellow	150 to 300
Green	235 to 470

A few transistors which have Pro Electron type numbers have a "K" or "L" suffix letter. This has nothing to do with gain grouping, and indicates that a different leadout configuration has been used. This method seems to have fallen from favour, and these days it would seem to be normal for devices having different leadout configurations to be given new type numbers, rather than modified versions of old ones.

JEDEC Codes

JEDEC stands for "Joint Electronic Device Engineering Council", and it is an American organisation. Devices having JEDEC type numbers accordingly have their origins in the U.S.A. These components are quite common in the U.K. though, and the JEDEC 1N and 2N series type numbers will be familiar to many readers (e.g. 1N4148 and 2N2926). These type numbers provide very little information about the components, but do have some significance. The number at the start of a JEDEC code is equal to one less than the number of leadout wires that the component possesses. It therefore gives some indication of the device type, as detailed here.

1	A diode or other two lead device
2	A bipolar, unijunction, or field effect transistor, or some form of S.C.R.
3	A dual gate f.e.t. or other four lead type
4 or 5	Opto-isolator

The second digit is always an "N", and is followed by a number having up to four digits. Devices are numbered in sequence as they are registered, and the type numbers give a rough guide to the relative ages of devices. A very few devices having "A" suffixes are available, and this simply indicates that they are improved versions of the original device. For instance, the 2N706A is an improved version of the earlier 2N706, and has a substantially different set of parameters.

JIS Codes

JIS (Japanese Industry Standard) type numbers would seem to be something of a rarity in U.K. electronic component catalogues. Japanese transistors, diodes, etc. do not seem to find their way into many designs for the U.K. home constructor. The first digit of the type number indicates the number of leadout wires in much the same way as the initial digit in a JEDEC type number (i.e. the number is one less than the number of leadout wires). The next two digits are letters which indicate the general type of the component. This is a list of the letters and the types of component they represent.

SA	PNP transistor or Darlington pair (high frequency)
SB	PNP transistor or Darlington pair (low frequency)
SC	NPN transistor or Darlington pair (high frequency)
SD	NPN transistor or Darlington pair (low frequency)
SE	Diodes
SF	SCRs (thyristors)
SG	Gunn diodes
SH	Unijunction transistors
SJ	P channel f.e.t.s (including power f.e.t.s)
SK	N channel f.e.t.s (including power f.e.t.s)
SM	SCRs (triacs)
SQ	Light emitting diodes
SR	Rectifiers
SS	Signal diodes
ST	Avalanche diodes
SV	Variable capacitance diodes
SZ	Zener diodes

The final part of the type number is a serial number of up to four digits in length. You may occasionally encounter JIS devices which have an extra letter at the end of the type number. This apparently indicates that the device has been approved by a Japanese organisation. An "N" for instance, indicates that it has been approved by a broadcasting station. Note that on actual devices the first two digits often seem to be absent. This is not particularly important since the first digit can be ascertained by counting the leadout wires, and the second digit is invariably an "S". There is only a risk of confusion if you fail to realise that the type number is of the abridged JIS variety.

Manufacturers' Digits
Not all semiconductors conform to any of these methods of numbering, and some are sold under manufacturer's own type

numbers. The first two to four letters then indicate the manufacturer concerned, plus (possibly) some general indication as to the type of device concerned or its encapsulation. This is a list of the main manufacturers and their code letters.

MJ	Motorola (metal cased power transistor)
MJE	Motorola (plastic cased power transistor)
MPS	Motorola (plastic cased low power transistor)
MRF	Motorola (high frequency or microwave transistor)
RCA	RCA
RCS	RCA
TIP	Texas Instruments (plastic cased power transistor)
TIPL	Texas Instruments (planar power transistor)
TIS	Texas Instruments (low power transistor)
ZT	Ferranti
ZTX	Ferranti

Opto-Components

Probably the most familiar opto semiconductor these days is the light emitting diode (l.e.d.). Basically a l.e.d. is just an ordinary diode, and it provides a true diode action. Unlike a light bulb, a l.e.d. will only function properly if it is connected the right way round. The energy dissipated by ordinary diodes ends up as heat, but l.e.d.s are constructed from different semiconductor materials that produce shorter wavelengths. In the case of infra-red l.e.d.s for remote control applications, the light output is all in the infra-red region, and there is no output at frequencies that the human eye can detect. The cheapest visible light l.e.d.s produce mainly red light, which is usually filtered to give a more pure red colour (but some non-filtered types give a slightly orangy-red coloured light). Slightly more expensive types that produce orange, yellow, and green light are available. Blue l.e.d.s do actually exist, but I can not claim to have actually seen one. The price of these components has fallen somewhat over recent years, but we are still talking in terms of at least several pounds per device, which compares with a matter of pence each for the standard red variety. Red and infra-red l.e.d.s are mostly based on gallium arsenide, while other colours are manufactured using other gallium based substances. Note that as l.e.d.s do not operate by having any form of hot filament, and normally operate at quite cool temperatures, they do not have the limited operating lives associated with filament bulbs. They will normally provide many years of trouble-free service.

Obviously l.e.d.s are physically quite different to ordinary diodes. They generally take the form of radial lead components having a lens moulded into the opposite end to the one from which the leadout wires protrude. The most popular method of designating the polarity of a l.e.d. is to have a flat section on the case of the component or a shorter leadout wire to indicate the cathode lead. These methods seem to be something less than universal though, and I have encountered a number of l.e.d.s which have the anode as the shorter lead. In order to determine the polarity it is best to consult the manufacturer's or retailer's literature. Getting the polarity wrong is unlikely to cause any damage, and trial and error can be used if necessary.

From the electrical point of view l.e.d.s do not behave quite like germanium or silicon diodes. Their forward threshold voltage is quite high, and is typically about 1.8 to 2 volts. Their reverse breakdown voltage is quite low, and is typically about 7 volts.

Light emitting diodes are available in a variety of shapes and sizes these days. These include large types, and components that are intended for printed circuit mounting, and which butt together to effectively form one multi-l.e.d. display. This form of display is called a "bargraph", and bargraph l.e.d. displays are also available. These are mostly in the form of ten l.e.d. components having rectangular segments, and an encapsulation that will fit a standard 20 pin d.i.l. holder.

One of the most useful types of l.e.d. is the high brightness type. In fact there are several classes of high brightness l.e.d., with names such as "ultra-bright" and "super bright". Ordinary l.e.d.s tend to have quite low light output levels, and under bright ambient lighting it can be difficult to determine whether they are on or off! The high brightness types provide much higher light levels, and in some cases are more than ten times brighter than a "bog standard" component operated at the same current. This enables them to be used in situations where an ordinary l.e.d. would be inadequate.

95

It also enables a given brightness to be obtained from a lower supply current. One of the great advantages of l.e.d.s over filament bulbs is that they will operate at low power levels. They require an operating potential of only about 2 volts, and are mostly operated at a current of just a few milliamps. The power consumed by a l.e.d. is typically a mere 10 to 20 milliwatts. This enables them to be used in small battery powered equipment.

One of the more unusual forms of l.e.d. is the multi-coloured type. In fact there is more than one type of multi-coloured l.e.d., and the most simple type just consists of two l.e.d.s of different colours sharing the same encapsulation. They are connected to the two leadout wires with the opposite polarity. The colour of the light from the component is therefore dependent on the polarity of the input signal, with (usually) red and green being available. The more interesting form of multi-coloured l.e.d. has what are again two l.e.d.s in the same encapsulation, but with three leadout wires and the common cathode method of connection. By switching on one section or the other it is possible to obtain red or green light. By switching on both sections and varying the relative l.e.d. currents it is also possible to obtain a range of yellows and oranges as well!

Some l.e.d.s have a built-in constant current generator. A l.e.d. is normally driven via a current limiting resistor, and the correct value for this resistor depends on the supply voltage in use. The idea of a l.e.d. having an integral current regulator is that it can be used over a wide supply voltage range without the need for an external current limiting resistor.

An important form of l.e.d. display is the seven segment type. These have the seven (more or less) rectangular segments in a figure of eight pattern, and by switching on the appropriate segments it is possible to produce a reasonable representation of any digit from 0 to 9. It has to be admitted that the quality obtained using this system is not very good, but this type of display is perfectly readable nevertheless, and it can be implemented quite cheaply and easily. I suppose that the name is not entirely apt, since all the seven segment displays that I have encountered have actually had eight segments. The eighth one is the decimal point. The segments are given

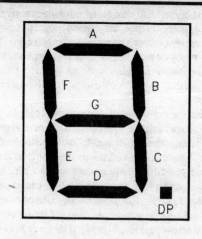

Fig.2.14 The segment identification letters used for seven segment displays

identification letters from "A" to "G" (plus "DP" for the decimal point), as can be seen from Figure 2.14. With seven segment displays either all the anodes or all the cathodes connect to a "common" ("COM") terminal. Circuits are designed to operate with one type of display or the other, and it is essential to obtain the correct type for the project concerned. Note that these displays are available in several sizes, and having more than one type of encapsulation and pinout arrangement. Unless you are designing your own board layout, you also need to make sure that you obtain precisely the right size and type of display, not just any common cathode or common anode type.

There is a relatively recent development in the form of dot matrix l.e.d. displays. A display of this type is simply a small panel having thirty-five l.e.d.s in a seven by five l.e.d. matrix, with the l.e.d.s connected together in the rows/columns configuration. With a suitable driver circuit a display of this type can display a full range of alpha-numeric characters. The display quality is not very good, and is comparable to some of the early and inexpensive dot matrix printers (which also used a five by seven matrix). It is good enough for many practical applications though.

Photo-Diodes

Diodes can be used to detect light as well as to generate it. In fact any diode will be affected to some degree by light, and normal diodes are protected from the ambient light level to prevent it from causing variations in their performance. An interesting but probably quite useless fact is that l.e.d.s, which are obviously not shielded from the ambient light, will work as light detecting diodes. Some photo-diodes are actually very much like l.e.d.s in appearance, and have a built-in lens to give them a narrow angle of view. Other types, particularly the infra-red detectors for use in remote control systems, have no built-in lens but instead have a large surface area in order to obtain good sensitivity over a wide angle of view. These have a variety of encapsulation types.

There are two basic operating modes for photo-diodes, one of which is the voltaic mode. This relies upon the fact that when subjected to light, a diode produces small electric currents. It has to be emphasised here that we are talking about very small currents indeed (usually no more than a few tens of microamps at a minuscule voltage), and normal photo-diodes are not suitable as a power source! The second mode of operation, and the one more commonly used, is the reverse biased mode. In this type of circuit the diode is reverse biased via a load resistor, and the leakage current varies in sympathy with the received light level. This generally gives somewhat better sensitivity than the voltaic mode of operation.

Photo-diodes, even the larger types, are not particularly sensitive. Their main advantage is that they can operate at relatively high speeds, and if used in the correct manner they can provide excellent linearity. In some applications high sensitivity is more important than speed and linearity considerations. A photo-transistor or a photo-darlington device is then likely to be a better choice. Again, there is no real difference between a photo-transistor and an ordinary type apart from the fact that one is shielded from ambient light and the other is not. In days gone by the OCP71 transistor was the standard photo-sensitive type, and it was basically just an OC71 in a transparent encapsulation. A popular ploy was to scrape the paint from the case of an OC71, effectively giving an OCP71 at a much lower cost. Later OC71s were filled with an opaque material that rendered this procedure unsuccessful, but it proves the point that there is no fundamental difference between a photo-transistor and an ordinary type.

The normal way of using a photo-transistor is as a light dependent resistor. The base terminal is ignored, and the collector to emitter resistance then varies in sympathy with the received light level. In effect, the leakage resistance of the component is governed by the light level it receives. A base bias can be applied to the device if desired, and will give a slightly higher operating speed. A darlington device is used in basically the same manner, but due to the amplification of the second transistor it will provide much higher sensitivity, albeit with a much reduced maximum operating speed.

Opto-Isolators
An opto-isolator is basically just a l.e.d. and a photocell of some type contained in a light-proof encapsulation. The light output of the l.e.d. is directed at the photocell. The basic idea is that activating the l.e.d. switches on the photocell. This enables a switching action to be transmitted through the device without any direct connection between the input and output circuits. The most common form of opto-isolator has an infra-red l.e.d. on the input side and a photo-transistor on the output side. Most types are guaranteed to withstand at least 2500 volts between the input and output sections of the component.

Opto-isolators of the type described above have their limitations, the main ones being a lack of efficiency and relatively low switching speeds. Many types offer an efficiency of only about 10% (i.e. the output current will only be about one-tenth of the input current), and can not handle frequencies of more than a few kilohertz. There are various improved types, including types which have a darlington pair on the output side. These offer very high efficiencies, but are only suitable for applications where a very low switching speed will suffice. Another form of improved opto-isolator has a photo-diode driving an emitter follower buffer stage which in turn drives a common emitter output stage. These offer a higher efficiency that is usually guaranteed to be about 100% or more. They also offer good switching speeds, although we are still talking in terms of an upper limit of a few hundred kilohertz rather than something into the mega-hertz range. However, this type of opto-isolator is adequate for most purposes.

There is a relatively recent and useful form of opto-isolator that has a triac on the output side. The light from the l.e.d. on the input side of the device causes leakage currents in the triac that trigger it, very much as if it had been triggered by a gate current in the normal way. Some of these opto-isolators can only handle quite modest currents, but they can be used to control a high current triac where higher power levels must be controlled.

Pyro Sensors

Pyro sensors have been in existence for many years, but it is only relatively recently that they have become readily avail-able to the amateur user. These components are a form of infra-red sensor, but they operate in a different part of the spectrum to normal infra-red detectors. Most semiconductor photo-sensors have optimum sensitivity in the infra-red part of the spectrum, and only a few special types peak in the visible part of the spectrum or into the ultra-violet region. Although most photo-diodes etc. peak at infra-red frequencies, their peak is at relatively short wavelengths that are only just out-side the visible part of the spectrum. To be more precise, they mostly peak at a wavelength of about 900nm.

Pyro sensors operate at much longer wavelengths of around 2 to 20μm. Their main applications are such things as intruder alarms and automatic doors. They are used to detect the body heat of an intruder and set off an alarm, or to detect someone as they approach a door so that the automatic opening mechanism can be activated before they reach the door. In applications of this type there can be difficulties in the body heat being quite low relative to the background level. Practical systems normally operate in conjunction with special lenses that give the system numerous alternate zones of high and low sensitivity. Anyone passing through the area covered by the system will pass through these zones, generating a varying output from the pyro-sensor. These systems are therefore dependent on the person moving through the area of coverage in (more or less) the right direction.

Pyro sensors are not normally semiconductor devices, but are based on a special ceramic material, such as lead zirconate titanate. A slice of the material is fitted with electrodes on opposite faces, and the heating caused by received infra-red rays produces small opposite charges on the electrodes. This is similar to the more familiar Piezo electric effect, which produces small electrical signals across the electrodes when a slice of suitable material is physically distorted (a property which is exploited in crystal and ceramic microphones and pick-ups). In both cases the signals produced are at a high impedance. Practical pyro sensors usually include a f.e.t. preamplifier stage which gives the device as a whole a fairly low output impedance. Some pyro sensors have two sensing elements connected in anti-phase. This helps to avoid problems with the background infra-red level causing spurious output signals.

The bandwidth of these components is strictly limited. Although they are made very thin so that they will be quickly heated by any received infra-red radiation, the upper limit of the frequency response is unlikely to be much better than about 2Hz or 3Hz! The response at the other end of the spectrum is limited by the load resistance placed on the sensor by the f.e.t. buffer amplifier. This resistance provides a discharge path for the charges generated by the sensor, and will eventually leak them away. The preamplifier will have a high value input bias resistor in order to give a reasonable low frequency response, but the lower limit is usually at about 0.2Hz. Although the bandwidth is very limited, it is well matched to presence detection applications, which are the only ones that this type of component are normally used for.

L.C.D.s

Liquid crystal displays (l.c.d.s) are another type of component that are worthy of mention here, even though, strictly speaking, they are not semiconductor components. The theory of liquid crystals is complex and confusing. Looking at things in highly simplified terms, the liquid crystal material is held between two transparent electrodes. Normally the rod-like crystals are in the "relaxed" state, which means that they are perpendicular to the electrodes, and allow a light to pass through with little attenuation. Placing a small voltage across the electrodes (with either polarity) results in the crystals shifting so that they are parallel to the electrodes. They then largely block light from passing through the component.

In a practical l.c.d. there is usually a reflective panel behind the component. This gives a pale colour when a display segment is relaxed, or an almost black colour when a segment is activated. The standard arrangement is therefore to have black segments on a pale greyish background. In the main, the early l.c.d.s were not very good. The contrast between activated segments and the background was quite low, the displays were only readable over a fairly narrow range of viewing angles, and contamination of the liquid crystal material often resulted in quite short operating lives. So-called twist and super-twist displays have improved the contrast and range of usable viewing angles, while refinements in manufacturing methods have resulted in longer operating lives. Most l.c.d.s are guaranteed to operate for five years or more, and most seem to be perfectly serviceable after ten years.

There are some quite complex l.c.d. displays for use in televisions, computer displays, etc., but the types you are likely to use in electronic projects are the 3½ and 4½ digit types. The half digit is a leading type which is either blanked or displays a "1", and can not display any other digits. Thus, a 3½ digit display can provide a maximum reading of 1999. Most l.c.d.s seem to include decimal points, positive ("+") and negative ("−") signs, and often other segments such as "Low Batt" warning types. As far as I am aware, single digit l.c.d.s are not available.

The main attractions of l.c.d.s when compared to l.e.d. displays are that they require very little operating power, and they are easily read under bright ambient lighting. Their main disadvantages are that they are not readable under dark conditions without the aid of a backlight, they need special and well designed driver circuits, and they can not normally be multiplexed. The special driver circuits are needed because the drive signal must be an a.c. type having no significant d.c. content. A d.c. signal will actually operate the display, but even a low d.c. signal level will cause problems with an electrolytic action that will rapidly result in the failure of the display. The drive signal is a fairly low frequency a.c. type (usually about 50Hz to 100Hz), and this makes multiplexing multidigit displays impractical. Although l.c.d.s are in some ways awkward to use, their low drive current of typically under a milliamp for a 3½ digit display makes them ideal for applications such as portable multimeters, digital thermometers, etc.

Chapter 3

INTEGRATED CIRCUITS

With transistors being manufactured in large numbers on chips of silicon and then diced up into individual components, I suppose that the obvious next step was to process the slice of silicon further so that the transistors were grouped into complete circuits. Instead of producing two thousand individual transistors from a slice of silicon, why not process it further to give (say) a hundred circuits each comprised of twenty interconnected transistors? For that matter, why not process the chip to produce a complex circuit having two thousand transistors? Although this may be an obvious next step, there are practical difficulties to overcome, and it was some time before fully operational integrated circuits were produced commercially in large numbers.

One problem that had to be overcome was the low yield of functioning transistors. If you are producing individual components, and only half of them on the slice of silicon actually work, you simply discard the bad half and proceed with the manufacture of the others. You will still obtain a large number of transistors per silicon slice, and production of the transistors will be economic. With the transistors grouped together in large numbers, and only fifty percent of the transistors actually operational, the chances of producing functioning devices becomes quite small. The larger the number of transistors per group, the lower the number of functioning devices that will be produced. With complex circuits, the number of individual transistors per silicon slice that fail needs to be very low, or the number of fully operational devices produced would be extremely low (or even none at all!).

There is no magic solution to this problem, and it is mainly by steadily refining manufacturing processes that component yields have improved, and highly complex devices have become a practical prospect. Even so, for devices that are the equivalent of a few hundred thousand or more components, the "dud" rate can be (and often is) extremely high. This largely accounts for the high cost of these devices. It might be necessary to manufacture ten or more devices for each one that is usable. The manufacturing process is often broken up into lots of separate units, rather than having one large production line. If disaster should strike one unit, and all the devices produced should be "duds", hopefully the other units would carry on normally. This makes it highly unlikely that a manufacturing plant of this type would have periods when no functioning devices at all were being produced. The interiors of the manufacturing plants have to be kept scrupulously clean. As few people as possible actually enter the clean zones, and they are only allowed to enter if they have been scrubbed suitably clean and are wearing special clothing to prevent specks of skin etc. from contaminating the manufacturing area.

Obviously few (if any) practical circuits consist of transistors, diodes, and no other components. In most cases large numbers of resistors and capacitors are needed, plus perhaps, a few inductors, switches, etc. Some components, such as switches and loudspeakers, clearly could not be fabricated on the chip of silicon together with transistors and diodes. There will probably always be the need for some discrete components, even if these amount to nothing more than a battery and a light bulb. Some components can be fabricated on the chip though, and with modern integrated circuits the discrete component count is often quite low.

Resistors can be produced on the chip quite easily, with a little processing of the silicon. The main problem is that high values tend to be difficult and expensive to produce in this way. One option is to simply put up with the added expense, but more usually any high value resistor would be a discrete type. The other, and much used alternative, is to simply design out any high value resistors. If you look at the internal circuits of integrated circuits you will usually find some rather strange looking arrangements that seem to use large numbers of components to achieve quite simple tasks. In particular, you will often find bias circuits that are comprised of a resistor feeding into long strings of forward biased diodes. You need to bear in mind that an arrangement such as this will provide accurate and stabilised bias levels, and adding a few extra diodes to an integrated circuit is not likely to have much effect on the cost of production. The circuits are designed to use components that can be produced on the chip cheaply, and to, as far as reasonably possible, eliminate components that either can not be produced on the chip, or which would be expensive to produce in this way.

Capacitors can be fabricated, but only small values of a few tens of picofarads or less are a practical proposition. Capacitors are actually something of a rarity in integrated circuits, but are to be found in a few, including internally compensated operational amplifiers such as the standard μA741C type. Large capacitors either have to be included in the form of discrete components, or designed out. In a transistor common emitter amplifier, instead of having an emitter resistor and a high value bypass capacitor, the circuit might have a low value resistor and a series of forward biased diodes.

It is not currently feasible to include worthwhile inductors in integrated circuits. These are normally included as discrete components, or new circuit techniques are used to make them unnecessary. A good example of this would be the integrated circuit stereo decoders for f.m. radio receivers. The early stereo decoders used $L - C$ filters to provide frequency doubling of the 19kHz pilot tone to the correct figure of 38kHz. Later designs used phase locked loops plus a divide by two circuit to give the same effect, and in most cases no inductors at all were required.

Common Collector

The main obstacle in producing integrated circuits, and one that took some time to defeat, was that all the transistors on a silicon chip using the normal manufacturing process have the substrate as the collector terminal. In other words, rather than having hundreds or thousands of individual transistors, there is effectively one huge transistor having hundreds or thousands of emitters and bases! The transistors only become fully independent devices once the piece of silicon has been diced up into individual chips.

There are two basic solutions to the problem, both of which we will consider here. These processes will only be considered in rather superficial terms since they are both extremely complex when it comes to the precise processes involved. One method is to start with a P type slice of semiconductor material. This is then processed to produce a layer of N type material on the top surface of the slice. This N type material is then processed in the normal way, producing transistors, diodes, etc., plus the necessary interconnections. The components can be isolated from one another simply by etching away the N channel material in the appropriate places.

This does leave a slight problem in that there is no direct electrical connection between the components, but they are all interconnected via the P channel substrate, and the P – N junctions formed between the substrate and the pieces of N type semiconductor. The solution to this problem is to connect the P type substrate to the negative supply rail of the completed integrated circuit. This ensures that the P – N junctions are all reverse biased, and the components on the chip are effectively in electrical isolation from one another.

There is a slight flaw in this system in that input signals to the integrated circuit might sometimes go negative of the negative supply rail. This leaves the risk of unwanted interconnections effectively being generated. It can actually produce problems with what are called "parasitic" transistors, which are transistors that are formed as an inevitable part of the manufacturing process, rather than by design. Normally these remain switched off and have no effect on the circuit. However, with negative input voltages they can be switched on, causing a malfunction of the device, or in an extreme case even causing a very large supply current to flow so that the device is destroyed. Integrated circuit data sheets normally give dire warnings if there are any potential problems with parasitic transistors.

The second method uses oxide insulation to isolate the components from each other. This process is based on a slice of N type semiconductor material which has vertical and horizontal grooves made using a diamond toothed saw. The finished slice of material is sometimes likened to a bar of chocolate, which I suppose has a similar appearance but on a massively larger scale. The top of the slice (i.e. the surface in which the channels are cut) is then oxidised, and a layer of polycrystaline silicon is grown on it. The slice is then turned over and ground down until separate regions of N channel material are exposed. Figure 3.1 helps to illustrate this sequence of events.

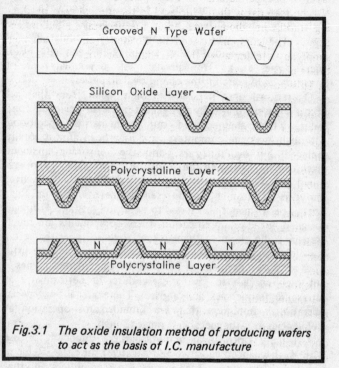

Fig.3.1   *The oxide insulation method of producing wafers to act as the basis of I.C. manufacture*

Turning this piece of silicon with its isolated N type regions into an integrated circuit is not a simple process. However, you can probably see that with these individual pieces of N type material on the chip it is possible to process them to produce individual transistors and other components. Further processing can then be used to provide the required inter-connections between the components.

Operational Amplifiers

With so many integrated circuits now available it is not possible to consider all of them in a publication of this type. Many integrated circuits are designed for a specific purpose. These "dedicated" chips may be usable in other applications, but in most cases they are not, or can only be used in this way if the circuit designer has a lot of determination and imagination. Here we will concentrate on the popular general purpose devices and families of integrated circuits (TTL digital types etc.). We will start with a popular form of linear integrated circuit; the operational amplifier.

Operational amplifiers derive their name from the fact that they were originally designed for use in analogue computers where they carried out mathematical operations. Although analogue computers have now been almost totally replaced by digital types, and the remaining analogue machines are mostly in the "museum piece" category, operational amplifiers seem to have steadily risen in popularity over the years. The number of different devices available and their level of performance also seems to be steadily rising. Although designed for d.c. amplification, these components are much used in audio circuits. Indeed, special audio types that offer low noise and distortion levels are available. They are little used at higher frequencies because the gain of most types is not high enough to give a useful level of performance at ultrasonic frequencies and above. There are a few special operational amplifiers that are intended for operation at frequencies into the megahertz range though.

Originally operational amplifiers were intended for use with dual balanced (positive and negative) supplies. Remember that they were intended for use as d.c. amplifiers, and that they could be required to produce negative as well as positive output levels (particularly when used in their intended role as the basis of analogue computers). Obviously most operational amplifiers are not used in applications of this type these days, and with suitable bias circuits the negative supply can often be eliminated. Even in d.c. circuits the negative supply may not be necessary. Some operational amplifiers can operate with their inputs and outputs right down to the 0 volt supply potential. If negative output voltages will not be needed, these

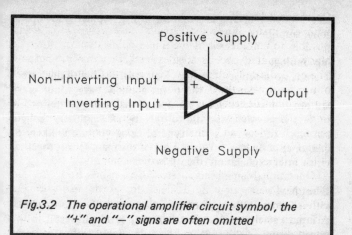

Fig.3.2 The operational amplifier circuit symbol, the "+" and "−" signs are often omitted

devices can be operated successfully with a single positive supply rail.

The normal circuit symbol for an operational amplifier is a triangle, as shown in Figure 3.2. The "+" and "−" signs respectively indicate the non-inverting and inverting inputs of the device. These are not always included though. Note that a triangle is often used as the circuit symbol for an integrated circuit amplifier of some kind, and is not used exclusively for operational amplifiers.

What is actually being amplified by one of these components is the voltage difference between the two inputs, and they are sometimes referred to as "differential" or even "voltage differencing" amplifiers. At d.c. and low frequencies the gain is very high − often at around 200000 times! This is called the "open loop" voltage gain. In practical circuits a negative feedback loop is used to reduce the voltage gain to a more usable level, and this is termed the "closed loop" voltage gain. The closed loop voltage gain and input impedance of the circuit can be set by two or three resistors, depending on the amplifying mode used (two resistors for the inverting mode and three for the non-inverting one). This makes circuit design relatively easy using these components. Repeatable performance is also relatively easy to obtain. These factors have probably been a large factor in the popularity of operational amplifiers.

Terminology
There is no shortage of terminology associated with operational amplifiers. Some of the terms actually have wider usage and are not strictly speaking operational amplifier terms. A lot of the jargon is specific to operational amplifiers though, and much of the rest is the type of thing you are unlikely to encounter elsewhere. This is a list of the main terms, together with a brief explanation of each one.

Offset Null
With a theoretically perfect operational amplifier, setting both its inputs at the central 0 volt supply level will result in the output assuming the same voltage. In practice offset voltages can often occur, the main consequence of which is an error in the output voltage. With a closed loop voltage gain of one the error is likely to be no more than a few millivolts. It is effectively amplified by the closed loop (d.c.) voltage gain of the circuit though, and at high gains the error can reach about one volt or even more. Where output errors caused by input offset voltages would otherwise be large enough to cause a malfunction of the circuit, an offset null control can be fitted, and used to trim out any error in the output voltage. This control normally consists of a preset resistor, or a preset resistor and one fixed value resistor. Offset null circuits tend to vary somewhat from one device to another, and in some cases (but mainly with multiple operational amplifier integrated circuits) there may be no provision for an offset null control at all.

Slew Rate
The slew rate of an operational amplifier (or any other circuit) is the maximum rate at which the output voltage can change. It is usually expressed as a change of so many volts per microsecond. It is an important factor with operational amplifiers that will be used at high frequencies, and by high frequencies I mean the upper end of the audio range or higher. The frequency response figures of operational amplifiers can tend to be a little flattering. They often suggest that a component is

112

perfectly usable at frequencies of a few hundred kilohertz or higher provided only low to moderate voltage gain is required. This may well be the case provided only small signal levels are involved. If large output voltage swings are required, the slew rate might prevent suitably large signals being produced. This is known as "slewing induced distortion", or just "SID" for short. Most modern operational amplifiers have much better slew rates than the early devices, and are very much less prone to this problem. Special high slew rate devices are available.

Large Signal Bandwidth
The large signal bandwidth is similar to slew rate, and is really just a different way of looking at things. It is the maximum frequency at which the amplifier can provide its maximum output voltage swing.

Common Mode Rejection
As an operational amplifier amplifies the voltage difference across its inputs, with a signal applied to both inputs there should be no change in the output voltage. In practice there will be a small imbalance, and some breakthrough at the output will occur. This parameter indicates how well a common input signal is suppressed at the output.

Latch-Up
Ideally, an operational amplifier would operate properly with its inputs at any voltages. Being more realistic, it should ideally operate properly with its inputs at any voltages within the supply levels. Practical devices sometimes fail to achieve this, and will only operate properly if the input voltages are within certain limits, and (or) the differential input voltage does not exceed a certain amount. Taking the input voltages outside the specified operating range is unlikely to result in any damage, provided these voltages are not outside the supply limits. The output of the amplifier will go fully positive or negative though, and may tend to stay in that state even if the input voltages are brought back within the acceptable limits. Switching off, waiting a few seconds, and then switching on again will normally restore normal operation. This "latch-up" as it is called, is not normally too much of a problem when an

operational amplifier is used in one of its standard amplifying modes, but it is a point that has to be kept in mind if it is used as a voltage comparator, or in some unusual circuit configuration.

Output Voltage Swing

The output voltage swing is the maximum positive and negative output levels that can be produced from a given supply voltage. This parameter is often specified with zero load on the output, but it may be given for a particular load impedance. Some modern devices can provide an output voltage swing virtually equal to the supply voltages. In particular, devices intended for operation using a single supply rail can provide output levels at virtually the negative supply voltage. With many devices the total output voltage swing is several volts less than the sum of the supply voltages. The standard μA741C type falls within this category.

Output Resistance

A theoretical operational amplifier has zero output resistance, but obviously this is something that is not achievable in practice. Typically the output resistance is quite low at about 75 ohms, and the application of negative feedback in a practical amplifier circuit can produce a closed loop output resistance of about one ohm. This could give the impression that operational amplifiers are power devices capable of providing quite high output currents. Apart from a few special types, this is not the case. Although the output impedance is quite low, and loading effects will normally reduce the output level by only a small amount, this only holds good for low to medium output levels, or for fairly high load impedances. At high signal levels with a low impedance load the output current limiting will come into action, and the output signal will be clipped.

Compensation

Although operational amplifiers have massive voltage gains at d.c. and low a.c. frequencies, the gain has to be rolled-off at frequencies of more than what is in most cases only about 10Hz or so. Without this reduction in gain at high frequencies

114

operational amplifiers would become unstable and would be totally unusable. Many operational amplifiers are internally compensated, which means that they do not require any discrete components to provide the high frequency roll-off. The internal compensation ensures that the device will not break into oscillation even when it is used with 100% negative feedback. Note that the internal compensation is merely guarding against instability due to positive feedback through the negative feedback circuit. In theory this should not occur, but in practice there are stray capacitances etc. which result in phase shifts, and can result in positive rather than negative feedback at some frequencies. The internal compensation will not necessarily be sufficient to prevent instability if a high gain, wide bandwidth circuit has a poorly designed layout that encourages stray feedback. Some operational amplifiers are internally compensated, but only for voltage gains of more than a certain amount (typically about ten times). For lower closed loop voltage gains a discrete compensation component or components will be needed. The amount of high frequency attenuation required depends on the closed loop voltage gain of the circuit, and the higher the voltage gain, the lower the amount of roll-off that is required. If high gain and a wide bandwidth are required, an externally compensated operational amplifier should be used. The improvement in high frequency performance can be quite dramatic. When used with a voltage gain of one hundred times, the standard μA741C operational amplifier has a bandwidth of just 10kHz. Using the externally compensated version (the μA748C) it is possible to obtain a bandwidth of about ten times this figure.

Gain Bandwidth Product

This is similar to the fT figure for a transistor. It is the frequency at which the open loop voltage gain of the component falls to unity. At lower frequencies the open loop voltage gain is proportionately higher. For example, if the gain bandwidth product is 1MHz, at 100kHz the gain will be ten times (1MHz (1000kHz) divided by 100kHz = 10). The closed loop voltage gain can never be more than the open loop voltage gain, and the gain bandwidth product places a definite

115

limit on the closed loop gain as well as the open loop variety.

There is insufficient space available here for masses of operational amplifier data, and this is not really intended to be a data book anyway. The list that follows gives the type numbers for most of the commonly available operational amplifiers, together with brief details of any special features they may have.

CA3130E	External compensation, ultra high input impedance MOS input stage, single supply operation.
CA3140E	Internal compensation, ultra high input impedance MOS input stage, single supply operation.
CA3240E	Duel version of CA3140E.
LF351	Low noise and distortion with high input impedance f.e.t. input stage, internally compensated.
LF353	Dual version of LF351.
LF347	Quad version of LF351.
LF411	Low input offset voltages, low drift, Jfet input stage.
LF412	Dual version of LF411.
LF441	Low power, Jfet input stage.
LF442	Dual version of LF441.
LF444	Quad version of LF441.
LM301	General purpose, external compensation.
LM308	Precision operational amplifier, externally compensated.
LM324	Quad operational amplifier, single supply operation.
LM358	Dual type, single supply operation, internally compensated.
LM1458C	Dual operational amplifier, internally compensated.
NE531	High slew rate, externally compensated.
NE5532	Dual low noise and distortion device.
NE5534	Low noise and distortion device.
OP-07C	Precision low noise operational amplifier.
OP-27G	Low noise, wide bandwidth, high slew rate, ultra low offset voltages (for instrumentation

	and high quality audio use).
RC4136	Quad low noise device.
TL061	Low current consumption, Jfet input stage.
TL062	Dual version of TL061.
TL064	Quad version of TL061.
TL071	Low noise, Jfet input stage.
TL072	Dual version of TL071.
TL074	Quad version of TL071.
TL081	General purpose, Jfet input stage.
TL082	Dual version of TL081.
TL084	Quad version of TL081.
μA741C	Industry standard compensated operational amplifier.
μA747C	Dual version of μA741C.
μA748C	μA741C without internal compensation.

Derivatives

There are devices that have similarities to operational amplifiers, but which do not, strictly speaking, fall within this category. An example of a device of this type is the LM3900N (or equivalent) quad Norton amplifier. This contains four current differencing amplifiers. Instead of the output voltage being governed by the relative input voltages, it is the input currents that are important with a device of this type. Norton amplifiers can not be used in standard operational amplifier configurations, but there are equivalent configurations that can be used. Although quite popular at one time, these are now used to a much lesser extent. They were originally designed to permit operational amplifier style circuits having a single supply rail to be produced. As this can now be achieved using "real" operational amplifiers such as the CA3140E and LM358, the attraction of Norton amplifiers has perhaps waned somewhat.

Operational transconductance amplifiers are an unusual but extremely useful form of operational amplifier. Like a Norton amplifier, they are current rather than voltage controlled devices. However, it is the output current and not the output voltage that is determined by the input signals. In many applications a load resistor is used at the output, effectively giving an output voltage that is governed by the input currents.

These devices have an additional input called the "amplifier bias input", and the output current is a function of the bias current and the relative input currents. The important point to note here is that the gain of the component can be controlled by the amplifier bias current. Adding a resistor in series with this input effectively gives voltage controlled gain. Operational transconductance amplifiers are therefore much used in voltage controlled amplifiers and filters. The CA3180E is a popular single type, while the LM13600N (and the almost identical LM13700N) are popular dual types. The CA3180E is a basic device, while the LM13600N and LM13700N contain an output buffer amplifier for each transconductance amplifier.

Operational amplifiers can be (and often are) used as voltage comparators. In other words, each input is used to monitor a voltage, and the output goes high or low depending on which voltage is the greater. There are devices specifically designed for this application though, such as the LM710, MC3302, LM311, and LM319. The main advantage of using a true voltage comparator is that these components usually have output stages that can switch at very high speeds. Of course, in many applications this is not an important factor, and an operational amplifier used as a voltage comparator may then be a cheaper and more practical solution.

Programmable operational amplifiers are an interesting but rare form of operational amplifier. They have a control input to which a bias current is fed. Using a low bias current gives a low level of current consumption, but the bandwidth of the device will then be relatively low. Using a high bias current gives higher current consumption and a wider bandwidth. This enables the current consumption to be set at the minimum level commensurate with the required bandwidth. Operational amplifiers of this type do not seem to be particularly popular, possibly due to their relatively high cost. I suppose that these are genuine operational amplifiers, as once they have been given a suitable bias current, they operate in all other respects just like conventional operational amplifiers.

Logic Devices
Digital integrated circuits probably represent the largest

category, with hundreds of logic devices readily available and in common use. These range from simple gates and inverters through to highly complex microprocessors containing the equivalent to more than a million components. Digital integrated circuits have just two valid output levels, called "logic 0" and "logic 1", but popularly known as just "low" and "high" respectively. Logic 0 is a low voltage that is typically about 0 to 1 volt. Logic 1 is a higher voltage that is generally about 4 to 5 volts. The acceptable voltage ranges for the two logic levels depends on the particular family of logic integrated circuits in use, the supply voltage, and possibly other factors. In the past it was not uncommon for logic circuits to have several supply voltages, including a negative supply, together with correspondingly strange logic levels. This type of thing is pretty rare these days though, and most logic circuits run on a single positive supply rail, with a 5 volt supply being by far the most common one.

Although I stated above that there are only two valid logic levels, you may well encounter references to "three state" or "tristate" outputs. The third state is a high impedance one where the output is effectively turned off. The idea is to have two or more outputs connected together, but with only one of them active at any one time. This enables several sources to drive an input or set of inputs in turn.

The most simple of the logic integrated circuits are the buffers, gates, and inverters. Figure 3.3 shows the circuit symbols for an inverter, a buffer, and various types of gate. For most logic elements there are no specific circuit symbols. On circuit diagrams they are just represented by the rectangle that is used as a general circuit symbol for integrated circuits, or for a section of an integrated circuit. Apart from gates which have about eight or more inputs, there is normally more than one buffer, inverter, or gate per integrated circuit. As a couple of examples, there would typically be six inverters or buffers per device, or four 2 input gates.

A buffer simply provides an output level that is equal to the logic level at the input. This may seem a bit pointless, but obviously there is a limit to the number of inputs that each output can drive. The number of inputs that can be driven is the "fanout" parameter. This figure is fifty or more

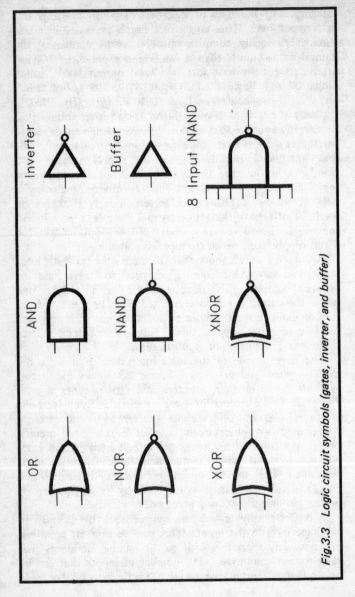

Fig.3.3 Logic circuit symbols (gates, inverter, and buffer)

for some families of digital integrated circuits, but is only about one-tenth of this figure for other families. Feeding an output to several buffers is a simple means of effectively increasing its fanout. There are high current buffers that permit higher than normal fanout levels to be achieved by a single output, but these are more normally used for driving high current loads such as l.e.d.s and relay coils. An inverter is much like a buffer, but the output has the opposite state to the input. Inverters can be used in buffering applications, or in a situation such as when a control signal is of the wrong polarity and it must be inverted in order to give one of the correct polarity.

Gates are a very simple form of decision making logic element, and must have at least two inputs. The output of a two input AND gate is high if input 1 and input 2 are high. Any other combination of input levels gives a low output level. A NAND gate is similar to an AND type, and is effectively an AND gate with an inverter added at the output. If input 1 and input 2 are high, the output will go low, but any other combination of input levels results in the output going high.

An OR gate has an output that goes high if either input 1 or input 2 is taken high. The output also assumes the high state if input 1 and input 2 are both high. A NOR gate is similar, but is effectively an OR gate with an inverter at the output. Thus, taking one or both inputs high sends the output low. There is an alternative (and little used) form of OR gate called the "exclusive OR", or "XOR" gate. This differs from the standard type in that taking both inputs high will not send the output high. The output will only go high if one input or the other is taken high, and I suppose that an XOR gate could reasonably be regarded as the true form of OR gate, since it provides an action that is more in keeping with the "OR" name. There is also an XNOR gate, which is effectively an XOR type having an inverted output.

We have been talking here in terms of two input gates, but a gate can have any number of inputs (but it must have at least two inputs of course). As an example, the output of a four input AND gate would go high if all four inputs were taken high, but would be low for any other set of input combinations.

Types which have more than two inputs operate under the same basic rules as their two input counterparts. A four input OR gate therefore has an output that goes high if any of its inputs are taken high.

Gates, and logic devices in general come to that, often have their function explained in data books with the aid of a "truth table". This is basically just a table which shows all the possible input states, together with the corresponding set of output levels for each one. This example truth table is for a three input AND gate.

Input 1	Input 2	Input 3	Output
LOW	LOW	LOW	LOW
LOW	LOW	HIGH	LOW
LOW	HIGH	LOW	LOW
LOW	HIGH	HIGH	LOW
HIGH	LOW	LOW	LOW
HIGH	LOW	HIGH	LOW
HIGH	HIGH	LOW	LOW
HIGH	HIGH	HIGH	HIGH

Truth tables for logic elements that have numerous inputs can be very long, and will often be abridged so that they provide only the important information. Even in our simple 3 input AND gate example, the truth table represents a rather verbose way of showing the function of the device, although it does have the advantage of showing its function in a manner that is unambiguous and immediately obvious.

With some components, such as flip/flips, a transition from the high state to the low state (or vice versa) on a certain input is of importance. With a transparent latch for example (which is a simple form of flip/flip circuit), the output assumes the same state as the input if the latching input is at one logic level, but it latches at its current state when the latching input is switched to the opposite state. Where a transition from one logic level to another is important for some reason, this will usually be indicated in the truth table, together with details of the effect of the transition.

122

Other Logic Blocks

Gates and buffers are just two of the many types of logic device currently available. Many of the logic integrated circuits you will find listed in component catalogues have rather specialised applications. A substantial percentage are of a more general nature though, and we will consider some of these common forms of logic device.

Flip/flops have already been mentioned, and there are various types to be found in the component catalogues. They fall into two main categories, which are the memory and divider types. Some are general purpose logic elements which can be connected to operate in either role. The divide by two type is the more simple of the two, and these simply provide one output pulse for every two input pulses. Often a series of divide by two stages are used to provide a range of output frequencies, or a circuit of this type can act as a binary counter. There are a number of these binary "ripple" counters available, and they often have a dozen or more stages per device.

With counters you will often encounter the terms "synchronous" and "asynchronous". For a straightforward divider chain there is a small delay through each section of the circuit. With high input frequencies and a long divider chain this can result in a significant delay between the input signal being applied, and all the outputs assuming valid states. This is not important in many applications, but in some it could cause a malfunction. In a synchronous counter there are circuits to equalise the delays through the device, so that the outputs are always properly synchronised with one another. There is still a delay between an input signal being applied and the outputs assuming valid states, but the delay is the same for every output. Counters (of whatever type) normally have a reset input, and taking this to the appropriate logic level results in all the outputs being forced low, taking the count back to zero.

The logic level needed to activate the reset input varies from one device to another. If an input is marked as just a plain "Reset" type, it is a logic 1 level that will activate it. If there is a line over the word "reset" on the pinout diagram, then it is a logic 0 level that is needed to activate the input.

Note that this is a general method of showing whether an input is active low (with the line) or active high (no line), and it does not just apply to reset inputs. This method is also used with outputs to show whether they go high (no line) or low (with line) when the device is activated. Obviously some inputs carry data which can be either high or low, and the line is not relevant in these cases (and will not be included on pinout diagrams). The input of a flip/flop for example, is the "Data" or "D" input. Flip/flops and other logic circuits often have complementary outputs (the "Q" and "negative Q" outputs).

When a flip/flop is used as a basic memory circuit, the input signal is applied to the data input, the output is taken from the Q output, and the latching pulse is applied to the "Clock" input. Depending on the type of flip/flop concerned, either a rising or falling edge on the clock input will latch the current logic input level at the data input onto the Q output. Often it is necessary to latch several "bits" of data simultaneously, and there are quad and octal flip/flops available, which will respectively latch four or eight bits at once. These are effectively four or eight independent flip/flops, but with their clock inputs taken to a common pin of the integrated circuit. There are some quite complex flip/flops that have a number of inputs, and which can be used in a variety of ways with the appropriate methods of connections. A detailed description of these goes beyond the scope of this book though.

Counters and Drivers
Binary counters are not the only types available. The main alternative is the decade counter, which can provide a divide by ten action as well as acting as a counter. In its basic form a decade counter has a clock input to which the input pulses are fed, a set of four outputs on which the count is produced (usually in binary coded decimal (b.c.d.) form), and a carry out output from which the divided by ten signal is available. This output is fed to the clock input of the next counter in a multi-digit type. Usually there will be other inputs, such as a reset type, and perhaps a gate input that can be used to effectively switch off the input signal if desired.

124

In order to fully understand binary and decade counters you need to have at least a basic understanding of binary arithmetic. An explanation of the binary numbering system goes beyond the scope of this book. Decade counters mainly operate with binary coded decimal, which is a slight variation on the standard binary scheme of things. Basically the idea is to have four logic outputs, with ten sets of logic states on these corresponding to decimal numbers from 0 to 9. With four outputs there are actually sixteen possible combinations of output levels, but six are left unused. This table shows the valid sets of output states, plus the digit each one represents.

D3	D2	D1	D0	Digit
0	0	0	0	0
0	0	0	1	1
0	0	1	0	2
0	0	1	1	3
0	1	0	0	4
0	1	0	1	5
0	1	1	0	6
0	1	1	1	7
1	0	0	0	8
1	0	0	1	9

The reason for using binary is that it makes the electronics easy to design. Simple two output level logic blocks are inexpensive and reliable in operation. The obvious drawback is that people operating digital equipment are conversant with the normal decimal numbering system, and require data to be entered into and obtained from the equipment in standard decimal form. This does not represent a major problem, and there are circuits which can take the numbers entered via a numeric keypad and convert them into their binary equivalents. There are also decoder circuits that can take a binary or b.c.d. signal and convert it into a standard decimal output. In the current context it is the seven segment decoders that are of primary interest. These take the output from a decade counter and display the corresponding digit on a seven segment l.e.d. display (see Chapter 2 for a brief explanation

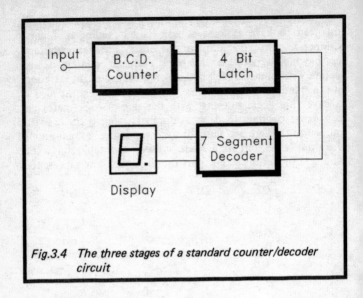

Fig.3.4 The three stages of a standard counter/decoder circuit

of seven segment l.e.d. displays).

A practical single digit counter usually consists of three logic blocks, as shown in Figure 3.4. First there is the counter itself, which registers the number of input pulses, and converts them to the corresponding b.c.d. code which is then placed on its outputs. The next stage is a four bit latch. This is not necessary in all applications, but it is generally better if the display can be left showing the last reading while a new count is under way. The idea is that as soon as a reading has been taken, the four bit code is placed in the latch and held there while the next reading is taken. The display then switches straight from one reading to the next, with the counting process not being evident to anyone viewing the display. In some applications the display could give rather misleading readings if the counting action was not hidden in some way. The rest of the circuit is a decoder which drives the appropriate display segments for whichever of the ten b.c.d. input codes is received. Note that the three circuit blocks do not necessarily appear in a circuit as separate logic integrated circuits. There are devices (such as the CMOS 40110BE)

126

that combine all three functions in a single chip, possibly with one or two extras such as a signal gate at the input.

Another popular form of counter/decoder is the "one of ten" type. In addition to a carry out output which provides a straightforward divide by ten action, there are ten other outputs. These are numbered from "0" to "9", and they each go high, in sequence, for one input cycle. This is a rather crude form of counter, but it is surprising how many times a device of this type proves to be invaluable in the control logic section of a digital circuit. The CMOS 4017BE one of ten decoder appears in a substantial number of projects for the home constructor. There is also an octal version of this component (the 4022BE) which provides a divide by eight function and has eight decoded outputs.

Line decoders have similarities to one of ten and one of eight decoders, but they have no built-in counter circuit. They activate an output, and which output this is depends on the binary code fed to the inputs. A binary counter plus a suitable line decoder would in fact give a one of ten or one of eight decoder of the type described previously. However, line drivers do not seem to be used in this manner very much. They are more normally used in place of a few gates. This simplified truth table for a three line decoder should help to explain the function of these devices.

Input 2	Input 1	Input 0	Output Activated
0	0	0	0
0	0	1	1
0	1	0	2
0	1	1	3
1	0	0	4
1	0	1	5
1	1	0	6
1	1	1	7

This gives tremendous versatility. It is possible to decode any set of input states by using the appropriate output. Furthermore, several sets of conditions on the same set of inputs can be detected by using more than one output. A line decoder can often replace a fairly complex gate arrangement, although it has to be admitted that where very high speed

127

operational is required it will often be better to use a set of gates to provide the decoding.

Tristate Buffers Etc.

A tristate buffer is merely one that has an output that can be switched to a high impedance state. The logic level on a control input determines whether the output is active or in the high impedance state. Practical tristate buffer integrated circuits normally have about four buffers per device. In some cases there are eight buffers per device, but there is then usually a common control input for all eight buffers. Like ordinary buffers, the tristate variety can be inverting or non-inverting.

A transceiver is similar to a buffer, but it is bidirectional. In other words, by altering the logic state on a control input, what were formerly the inputs become the outputs, and what were previously the outputs become the inputs. Usually the outputs, regardless of which set of terminals they happen to be at the time, are tristate types. These devices are mainly used as buffers in microprocessor based equipment, where their bidirectional properties are needed due to the use of a bidirectional data bus.

Some buffers are Schmitt Trigger types. Normally if the input voltage to a buffer is steadily increased the output will fail to respond at first, then it will move over to the opposite logic level fairly rapidly (but less than instantly), and further increases in the input voltage will then have no further effect. This lack of triggering from one logic level to the other will not usually cause any problems, since the input signal will almost invariably be a rapidly switching type. This leaves no risk of the output wavering at invalid logic voltages.

A Schmitt trigger buffer has a different type of transfer characteristic, where the output does trigger from one logic level to the other once a certain input threshold voltage has been reached. The input voltage at which the output will trigger back to the original state is lower than the initial trigger voltage. This "hysteresis" as it is called, is deliberately introduced in order to prevent spurious output pulses from being generated as the input signal goes through the transition level, even if the input signal changes slowly and contains a certain amount of noise.

128

Last, and by no means least, mention should be made of shift registers. The basic idea of a shift register is to have a number of parallel inputs, and a serial output. The data fed to the parallel inputs is latched into the device. It is then transmitted from the serial output, literally bit-by-bit, under the control of a clock signal fed to clock input of the device. For example, if the data fed to the parallel inputs is 1100, on the first clock pulse the output will be low, it will be low again on the next clock pulse, and then high for the next two clock pulses. Most shift registers seem to be able to operate the other way round, and can have data clocked in on the serial input, with it then being available as parallel data on the parallel lines.

Logic Families

One of the more confusing aspects of logic integrated circuits is the large number of logic families currently in existence. This has resulted in what is fundamentally the same device often being available under several slightly different type numbers. Although the basic function may be the same, and their type numbers may be virtually identical, such groups of devices are not necessarily fully interchangeable. In fact in most cases they will not be fully interchangeable, and could have minimal compatibility.

The reason that the numerous logic families have come into being is that the original logic devices left something to be desired in terms of their overall performance. Some of these logic families (such as the DTL (diode transistor logic) and RTL (resistor transistor logic) types) have been obsolete for many years now. The two main survivors that now dominate the logic integrated circuit market are the TTL (transistor transistor logic) and the CMOS (complementary metal oxide semiconductor) type. The TTL name is derived from the fact that the output stage uses a transistor switch and another transistor as its load. The CMOS name is derived from the fact that these integrated circuits are based on complementary (P channel and N channel) MOS transistors.

TTL integrated circuits have the advantage of being able to operate at quite high speeds, but they have the disadvantage of a relatively high current consumption. In fact even a few simple gates require significant supply currents, and the large devices consume quite large amounts of power (getting noticeably warm in the process). These components are considerably less than ideal for battery powered equipment.

CMOS logic integrated circuits have very low levels of power consumption. The supply current is largely dependent on the operating frequency, and rises from practically zero at very low frequencies to something comparable to TTL types at high frequencies. However, as few (if any) logic circuits have every device running flat out continuously, practical CMOS circuits tend to have very much lower levels of current consumption than TTL equivalents. Although CMOS devices might seem like an ideal solution, their weakness is that they will not operate at really high frequencies. In fact some devices when operated at low supply voltages will not operate properly at frequencies of more than about 2MHz!

These deficiencies in standard TTL and CMOS logic devices led to the development of numerous improved versions, offering lower current consumption, higher operating speed, or both. The standard TTL integrated circuits now have to be regarded as obsolete, and are little used in new designs. The same is not really true of the standard CMOS range, which is still much used today. The original "A" suffix devices have been superseded by a slightly improved "B" series, which have better static protection and improved output stages. There are also a few "UB" devices which lack the output buffer stages. These are still basically the same devices though, and except when a few types are used in unusual ways, they have total compatibility with the original "A" series components. Their relatively low maximum operating speed is obviously a limitation, but where high speed is of no importance, their low current consumption, wide supply voltage range (3 to 18 volts), and low cost makes them the obvious choice.

For high speed operation it would obviously be better to have components having much lower current consumptions than the standard TTL type, and preferably having a higher maximum operating frequency as well, so as to increase their versatility still further. What I suppose has to be regarded as the new standard type of TTL logic integrated circuit is the low power Schottky type. These have the standard 74**

130

series type numbers, but with LS added after the "74" part of the type number (e.g. 74LS00). They are pin for pin equivalents to the original devices, and are largely compatible with them. Due to their slightly different characteristics, they do not have unconditional compatibility with the standard 74** series devices.

In particular, the drive current available from an LS TTL output is lower than that from an ordinary TTL output. Provided a circuit is based entirely on LS devices this will not matter, as they require lower input currents than the standard devices. This gives LS TTL devices a higher fanout figure than the ordinary TTL variety. Fanout, as explained previously, is simply the number of inputs that an output can drive reliably, and is ten for ordinary TTL devices, and twenty for the LS TTL type. A standard 74 series device can drive some twenty LS TTL types, but a LS TTL type can only drive five standard TTL inputs reliably. Some caution needs to be exercised if an LS TTL integrated circuit is to be used as a replacement for a standard TTL type.

Building circuits based entirely on LS TTL devices should give few difficulties, since virtually every standard TTL device is now available in an LS version. The LS devices are slightly faster than the standard TTL equivalents, but typically require only about one-fifth as much power. This improved performance is obtained by having Schottky diodes at strategic points in the circuits. These diodes have lower forward threshold voltages than normal silicon diodes, and they are used to prevent certain transistors from being biased into saturation. This avoids slow switch-off times due to storage effects, and enables much faster operation to be obtained from a given supply current.

There are other Schottky series integrated circuits, including the standard type which have an "S" in the type number instead of "LS" (e.g. 74S00). These are designed to provide high speed operation rather than giving lower current consumptions than the standard TTL range. The increase in speed is quite significant, with maximum operating frequencies that are typically about three to four times those of the standard TTL components. Another form of Schottky TTL integrated circuit is the "Advanced Low Power Schottky" type, which have the letters "ALS" in the type number (e.g. 74ALS00). At one time it looked as though these would become the most popular form of TTL integrated circuit, but they never seemed to become dominant, probably because relatively few applications really required their higher performance and merited the higher cost. This range has slightly higher operating speed than the ordinary LS range, but only requires about half the supply current. There is also an "Advanced Schottky" range which have the letters "AS" in the type number (e.g. 74AS00). These are intended as a rival to the ordinary Schottky range, but offer higher operating speeds at about the same level of current consumption.

High Speed CMOS

Most of the recent developments in logic integrated circuits seem to centre around CMOS types. However, these have levels of performance that are well beyond those of the traditional CMOS types. In fact most of these components are offered as pin compatible versions of components from the TTL range, rather than as improved 4000BE series components. These devices are not fundamentally different to the original CMOS type, and are produced using what is a more refined version of the original technology, rather than totally new processes.

The original 74 series CMOS devices (the 74C00 etc.) were just ordinary CMOS devices internally, but they had functions and pinouts which matched components in the TTL range. They offered no improvement in performance over ordinary CMOS components, and were largely incompatible with TTL devices. They were designed primarily to make it easy for electronic engineers who were familiar with TTL integrated circuits to design CMOS based logic circuits. This range of components never seemed to gain much popularity, and would now seem to be obsolete.

The standard improved CMOS family is the "High Speed CMOS" type, and these have the letters "HC" in the type number (e.g. 74HC00). There is an alternative type which has "HCT" in the type number, and these differ from the standard high speed CMOS devices in that they have a narrower supply voltage range (4.5 volts to 5.5 volts as opposed to 2 volts to 6 volts), and their inputs and outputs operate at standard TTL logic levels. These components could take over from the low power Schottky type as the new standard TTL family, and they would seem to be rising in popularity. Their only real drawback is that their cost is relatively high at present, although the difference in cost is not very great in some cases.

High speed CMOS components offer a very high level of performance. They will operate at frequencies of up to about 60MHz, which makes them about twice as fast as standard TTL devices. They have the high input impedances associated with CMOS components, but can provide output currents nearly equal to those of other TTL families. They can drive two ordinary TTL inputs, ten LS TTL inputs, and what for practical purposes can be regarded as an infinite number of high speed CMOS inputs. Like ordinary CMOS logic integrated circuits, the high speed type have a level of power consumption that is largely dependent on the operating frequency. At very high frequencies they have a current consumption that is comparable to LS TTL components, but at low frequencies they consume very little power at all. In most practical circuits this produces a massive reduction in current consumption compared to any other form of TTL device.

It is worth noting that the high speed CMOS ranges include equivalents to both TTL and the 4000BE series CMOS devices. The 74HC4001 for example, is the high speed CMOS version of the 4001BE quad 2 input NOR gate.

There are several other TTL families, but you are unlikely to encounter devices from these. One of these ranges is the "FACT" type, which is the "Fairchild Advanced CMOS Technology" range of components. These have current consumptions that are comparable to the standard high speed CMOS types, but they achieve about double the operating speed and have higher maximum output currents. This range could well become quite popular in the future.

Other ranges include the high speed one, which has 74H00 series type numbers, and the "FAST" ("Fast Advanced Schottky TTL") range. The first of these is a high current consumption high speed range. The second range has a lower current consumption and higher operating speed than the standard Schottky range. The low power TTL components (which have 74L00 series type numbers) now seem to be obsolete. These have lower current consumptions than the standard TTL devices, but are much slower in operation. Probably their demise was as a result of the 4000BE series components offering superior results in most of their potential applications. Finally, there is a family of logic integrated circuits called "ECL" ("Emitter Coupled Logic"), and these offer the ultimate in high speed operation. However, they are quite expensive, require dual supply rails, and are not available as pin compatible TTL or CMOS equivalents (which would be impossible anyway due to their unusual supply requirements).

Obviously it is possible to utilize various TTL families in the same circuit, and under some circumstances it might even be possible to mix TTL and 4000BE series CMOS types successfully. Equally obviously, due to variations in the valid input/output voltage ranges, and differences in input/output currents, mixing logic families has the potential to produce malfunctions. Unless you really know what you are doing it is advisable not to mix these components. The exception is when you have what might be a suitable component in the spares box. Trying it out in practice to see if it will give satisfactory results is unlikely to cause any damage, and it might even work perfectly in the circuit.

The table on page 135 shows some of the key figures for several ranges of logic integrated circuit, and gives a good indication of the compatibility between families (or the lack of it).

The fanout figures are the number of standard TTL inputs that can be driven. CMOS devices can operate over a wide supply voltage range, and the maximum output current is largely dependent on the supply voltage used. The output current figures in the table are for a 5 volt supply. Similarly, the input and output voltage figures are for a 5 volt supply. The relative power consumption figures are only intended as a rough guide, as the current consumption of all these components (but particularly the three CMOS types) vary considerably with changes in the operating frequency. These

	CMOS	TTL	LS TTL	74HC	74HCT
Supply Voltage	3–18V	4.75–5.25V	4.75–5.25V	2–6V	4.5–5.5V
D.C. Fanout	1	40	20	10	10
Output Current (H/L)	2.1/0.45mA	16/0.4mA	8/0.4mA	4/4mA	4/4mA
Maximum Low Input	1.5V	0.8V	0.8V	0.9V	0.8V
Minimum High Input	3.5V	2V	2V	3.15V	2V
Maximum Low Output	0.05V	0.4V	0.5V	0.1V	0.1V
Minimum High Output	4.95V	2.4V	2.7V	4.9V	4.9V
Typical Maximum Frequency	5MHz	35MHz	40MHz	40MHz	40MHz
Relative Power Consumption	0.002	1	0.2	0.002	0.002

figures assume that devices are operated at low to medium frequencies, or intermittently at high frequencies. The maximum operating frequency ratings are also only intended as a rough guide. The actual figure varies significantly from one device to another, with the more simple devices generally able to operate at slightly higher frequencies than the complex ones.

135

Voltage Regulators

The three terminal monolithic voltage regulators must rank as one of the most popular ranges of integrated circuits. They are used in the manner shown in Figure 3.5. This is for a positive regulator, but the negative types are used in essentially the same way. The polarity of the input and output voltages are reversed though. The only discrete components required are decoupling capacitors at the input and output of the circuit. These are needed to prevent instability, and they should be mounted as close to the voltage regulator as possible. The only major drawback of these components is that they do not include a facility for varying the output voltage, but they are available in a variety of voltage ratings, including most of the popular supply voltages.

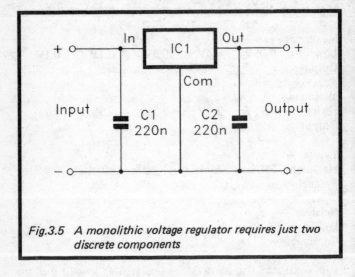

Fig.3.5 A monolithic voltage regulator requires just two discrete components

Although very simple to use, these components are actually quite sophisticated series voltage regulators that offer a very high level of performance. The exact performance figures vary somewhat from one type to another, but these are some typical figures. Load regulation is approximately 0.25% (i.e. variations in the load current produce variations in the output

136

voltage of less than 0.25%). Line regulation is better than 0.1% (i.e. variations in the input voltage produce variations at the output of less than 0.1%). The output noise voltage is only around 75 microvolts, and the ripple rejection is about 70dB. The dropout voltage is 2 volts for the 5 volt types, and 2.5 volts for all the other output voltages. The dropout voltage is simply the minimum voltage difference between the input and output voltage that will provide proper operation of the regulator. The 2 volt dropout voltage of a 5 volt component for instance, means that it will only function properly if the input voltage is at least 7 volts (the 5 volt output voltage plus the 2 volt dropout voltage).

These components are protected against short circuits or other overloads on the output by a built-in current limiting circuit. This is of the fold-back variety. In other words, in the event of an overload, rather than simply limiting the output current to no more than a certain figure, it is actually reduced as the overload is increased. With a 1 amp regulator a minor overload might cause an output current of about 1.1 amps, whereas with a short circuit the output current might only be around the 300 milliamp mark. This gives improved protection against prolonged overloads. This type of overload can result in the regulator eventually overheating due to the high dissipation with a short circuit or very low resistance across the output. By reducing the output current to only about one-third of the maximum level, the dissipation is kept down to a level where there is no danger of overheating.

Monolithic voltage regulators are not always sold under type numbers. They often seem to be advertised as something like a "12 volt 1 amp positive regulator". Where type numbers are used, they are $\mu A78**$ types for positive voltage regulators, and $\mu A79**$ types for negative regulators. Often the "μA" part of the type number is omitted. These basic type numbers are for the 1 amp regulators, and the two digit number at the end of the type number indicates the output voltage. As a couple of examples, a $\mu A7805$ is a 1 amp 5 volt positive regulator, and a $\mu A7915$ is a 1 amp 15 volt negative type. An "L" prior to the voltage number indicates that the device is a low power type, and these can handle output currents of up to 100 milliamps. Devices which have an "M" in the type number are medium power (500 milliamp types), and those with an "S" are high power (2 amp) components.

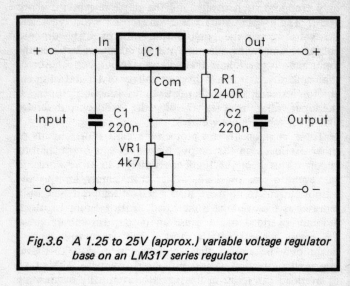

Fig.3.6 A 1.25 to 25V (approx.) variable voltage regulator
         base on an LM317 series regulator

Note that there is now an alternative type of three terminal monolithic voltage regulator. These are variable output voltage types, and are used in the circuit configuration shown in Figure 3.6. These regulators also offer a very high level of performance, and are ideal for many variable voltage supply applications. They are also useful if the required supply voltage is not available from an ordinary three terminal monolithic voltage regulator.

Chapter 4

THE REST

In this chapter we will consider a variety of passive components that do not fall within the three categories (resistors, capacitors, and inductors) that were covered in Chapter 1. There is a vast number of components that fall within this category, many of which are highly specialised in nature. Here we will only consider the more common examples.

Switches

Switches must rank as one of the most simple of electronic components, but even with these there is a great variety of types and a great deal of terminology associated with them. Terms such as s.p.s.t. can be a bit confusing for the uniniti- ated. There are four terms of this type, and Figure 4.1 should help to explain them. This shows the circuit symbol for each of the four types of switch.

The most simple is the s.p.s.t. (single pole single throw) type, which is just a basic on/off type switch. The d.p.s.t. (double pole single throw) switch is two on/off switches that are operated in unison. The s.p.s.t. type would be used for something like on/off switching in battery powered equip- ment, whereas the double pole type would be used for an application such as the on/off switch in mains powered equipment, where for safety reasons it is normal to switch both the "L" and "N" lines.

The s.p.d.t. (single pole double throw) type is a changeover switch. In other words the pole terminal can be switched to connect to one or the other of the other terminals. A switch of this type could, for example, be used to switch between two input sockets of an audio amplifier, so that the desired input could be selected using the switch. The d.p.d.t. (double pole double throw) switch is just two s.p.d.t. types operated by a common control. Taking our audio switching example, the double pole variety would be needed for a stereo amplifier, where there are two pairs of input sockets to switch between.

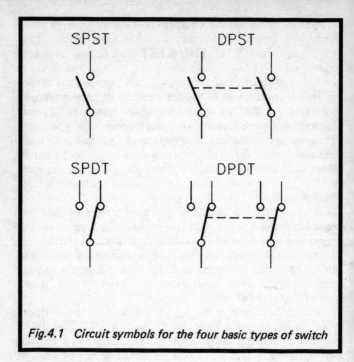

Fig.4.1 Circuit symbols for the four basic types of switch

These four basic types of switch are available in a variety of guises, one of which is the slider switch that will be familiar to most users of inexpensive cassette recorders, radios, etc. These are quite cheap, but some slider switches seem to be rather crude and probably do not have very long operating lives. Another common form of switch is the toggle type, which is operated via a lever. In the case of standard toggle switches this lever (sometimes called the "dolly") is quite large, but miniature and sub-miniature types are now available and are the more popular choice for modern equipment. Another common form of switch is the rotary type. These mostly have quarter inch diameter or 6 millimetre spindles that will take standard push-on or grub screw fitting control knobs.

Finally, there are push-button versions of these switches. These can be of the locking or non-locking varieties (also known as latching and non-latching push-button switches). With the non-locking type, pressing the push-button results in the switch changing over to its alternative positive, but as soon as the button is released the switch reverts to its original state. In fact the other types of switch can have this "biased" method of operation, but it is a rare option for toggle types, and something I have not encountered in rotary and slider switches. The locking push-button switches stay in the new state once they have been operated. To switch the component back to the original state it is operated a second time. In fact each time the switch is operated it will change state and latch in the new state. Push-button switches have different circuit symbols to other types. Figure 4.2 shows the symbols for simple s.p.s.t. switches of the normally closed and normally open types. As the names suggest, a normally open type is set to the "on" position when it is operated, whereas the normally closed type switches over from the "off" to the "on" position when it is operated.

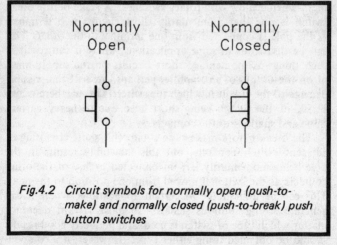

Fig.4.2 Circuit symbols for normally open (push-to-make) and normally closed (push-to-break) push button switches

Note that these switches are available with more than two poles. In some component catalogues you will find four pole changeover switches for example. Obviously it is possible to have switches with any desired number of poles, but in practice it is difficult to find components having more than four poles. Most projects are designed to use basic single and double pole types.

Multi-Way
There are two basic solutions to producing switches having more than two ways. The more simple of the two is the rotary type. Rotary switches are readily available in 12 way 1 pole, 6 way 2 pole, 4 way 3 pole, and 3 way 4 pole varieties. Modern rotary switches of this type invariably seem to be equipped with an adjustable end-stop mechanism. This enables the switch to be set for any desired number of ways from two to its maximum number of ways. If a five pole two way switch is needed for instance, a six pole two way type set for five way operation would fit the bill.

When dealing with rotary switches you will sometimes encounter the terms "make before break", and "break before make". These terms can actually be applied to any changeover or multi-way switch, but you are most likely to come across them when dealing with rotary switches. A make before break switch is one that momentarily short circuits two terminals as the pole is connected from one terminal to the other. This can be disastrous in some applications, where it can result in such things as momentary short circuits on the supply lines, or on the output of an amplifier perhaps. Apart from possible damage to the circuit in which the switch is fitted, there is also a risk of the switch being short lived due to heavy current flows and sparking at the contacts.

The break before make type avoids this short circuiting of adjacent switch contacts, but this inevitably results in the pole being momentarily left unconnected to any of the other contacts as the switch is moved from one position to the next. This can be undesirable in certain applications, where it can generate strong spurious signals. In most cases it does not matter which type of switch is used, and perfectly good results should be obtained using either type. However, if a components list specifies one type or the other, it is almost certainly very important that the correct type is used.

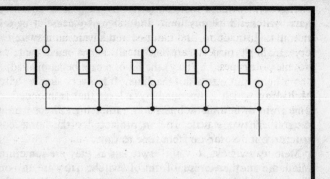

Fig.4.3 *Connecting a bank of five push-button switches to give a 5-way 1-pole action*

The alternative multi-way switch is a bank of interlinked push-button types. These generally work on the basis of any switch that is engaged being disengaged when another switch is operated. In other words, no more than one switch at a time can be in the "on" position. These switches are really individual types that do not provide true multi-way operation unless they are wired up correctly. Figure 4.3 shows how a bank of five push-button switches can be connected to provide five way single pole operation. Of course, if the switches have several poles, by connecting each set of poles in this way, a five way multi-pole type can be produced.

Banks of push-button switches are much used in commercial equipment for such things as waveband selectors in radio sets and input selectors in hi-fi amplifiers. They are relatively little used in designs for the home constructor though. One reason for this is probably the comparatively high cost. Also, using these switches tends to complicate the mechanical side of project construction. Their mounting requirements are much more awkward than the simple 10 millimetre diameter mounting hole required for an ordinary rotary switch. Where complex switches having a large number of ways or poles are required, this type of switch might prove to be the only available type that will provide the required contact arrangements.

The term "micro-switch" tends to suggest a switch of extremely small proportions, and seems to cause a certain amount of confusion. It does not actually mean a switch of very small physical dimensions at all, and a micro-switch is one that is operated by (say) the lid of a case being opened, or a coin being put into a slot machine. It is a very simple switch mechanism which is operated by a lever that is intended for some form of automatic operation, rather than direct manual control. They are little used in projects for the home constructor, but do crop up from time to time.

Mercury switches, or "tilt" switches as they are sometimes called, are another unusual form of switch. They are also one that is intended for some form of automatic operation rather than direct manual control. Figure 4.4 shows the basic arrangement used in this type of switch. It consists of a

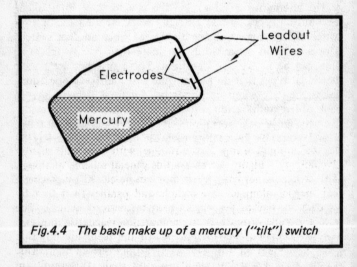

Fig.4.4 The basic make up of a mercury ("tilt") switch

container made from an insulating material and having two electrodes on the interior. The electrodes are connected to leadout wires or terminals on the exterior of the unit. There is a small amount of mercury in the container, and this is a metal which is molten at normal room temperatures. Being a

144

metal it is a very good conductor of electricity. At some angles the mercury will fail to bridge the two contacts, and the switch will be open. At other angles it will cover both electrodes, and the switch will be closed. The switch can therefore be turned on and off simply by tilting it to suitable orientations.

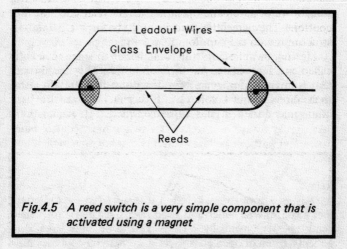

Fig.4.5   A reed switch is a very simple component that is activated using a magnet

Yet another unusual and little used form of switch is the reed type. This has two thin and springy pieces of metal (the "reeds") mounted in a glass envelope, with their ends slightly overlapping. Figure 4.5 shows this general scheme of things. The switch is normally open, but can be closed by placing a bar magnet alongside the switch, and parallel to it (not by placing one end of the magnet next to the reed switch). The effect of the magnet is to temporarily magnetise the two reeds. The two overlapping ends of the reeds are opposite magnetic poles, and they therefore attract one another. Due to the thinness and flexibility of the reeds, this results in them touching, and closing the switch. When the magnet is removed they no longer attract each other, and the springiness of the metal results in the separating. Removing the magnet thus opens the switch.

145

With all switches you need to keep in mind that they have voltage and current ratings that must not be exceeded. Also bear in mind that there are often power ratings which apply more stringent limits on the voltages and currents that can be handled by a switch. For instance, a switch might have voltage and current ratings of 250 volts and 5 amps respectively. The maximum power it can handle might only be 500 watts though. In other words, it can not handle the 250 volt and 5 amp levels simultaneously (which would be some 1250 watts). At 5 amps it could handle 100 volts (5 amps x 100 volts = 500 watts), or at 250 volts it could handle 2 amps (250 volts x 2 amps = 500 watts). Another point to watch is that the a.c. and d.c. voltage ratings are often markedly different. In many applications the power levels are insignificant, and this is a factor that does not need to be considered. It is something that should always be checked if a switch must control more than a few watts, or voltages/currents that are even moderately high.

Relays
A relay is a form of switch, but it is operated by a solenoid (i.e. a coil of wire which acts as an electro-magnet) rather than being operated manually. These used to be quite large components, often of open construction so that you could see how they worked. Modern relays are mostly quite small, and are enclosed in plastic cases which keep dust and dirt away from the delicate mechanisms. Relays usually have changeover contacts rather than simple on/off types, and in many cases there are several sets of contacts. Like ordinary switches, relay contacts have voltage and current ratings that must not be exceeded. The contact ratings of some components are quite low, and you need to carefully check this point when using a relay in any application where it is called upon to switch significant power levels.

Of equal importance are the ratings of the relay coil. The voltage quoted is the nominal operating voltage, and most types will operate on significantly higher and lower voltages. Most component catalogues list the true operating voltage range for each relay. The coil resistance should also be quoted, and this is another important figure. Some relays seem to have coil resistances of a few tens of ohms, while others have resistances of several hundred ohms. In general, using a type which has a higher coil resistance than that called for in a components list will not have any adverse effects. It will simply result in a lower current consumption, which could be beneficial in some cases (such as where a circuit is battery powered). Using a relay having a coil resistance more than marginally lower than the specified figure is a more dubious practice. The current through the coil could be far higher than the driver circuit and power supply are designed to handle. This could result in a malfunction of the circuit, or could even result in damage to some of the components. Note that apart from relay coils that are meant to be driven from the mains supply, most are only intended for d.c. operation. Due to the highly inductive nature of a relay coil, operation from an a.c. signal is likely to give unpredictable and unsatisfactory results.

There is an alternative and less well known form of relay called a reed relay. This is basically just a reed switch of the type described previously, but contained in a solenoid. A suitable current through the coil magnetises the reeds and closes the switch — removing the current causes them to spring apart again and open the switch. Relays of this type have the advantage of very high speed operation, and they will usually operate from quite low power levels. They have a serious drawback though, in that they can only handle quite low voltages and currents. Also, complex contact arrangements are only possible using several relays.

Speakers and Microphones, Etc.

Apart from a few special types for P.A. and hi-fi use, loudspeakers are of the moving coil type. These have a permanent magnet and a moving coil, and are sometimes referred to as "permanent magnet" rather than moving coil loudspeakers. Figure 4.6 shows the basic arrangement used in a loudspeaker. The way in which a loudspeaker operates is very simple indeed. With the signal fed to the voice coil with one polarity, the coil will be attracted onto the pole piece. With the signal of the opposite polarity, the magnetic poles of the speech coil and pole piece will be such that they will repel

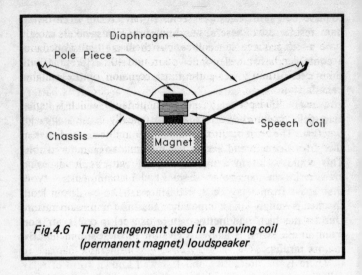

*Fig.4.6 The arrangement used in a moving coil
(permanent magnet) loudspeaker*

one another. Thus a varying a.c. input signal causes the speech
coil to move backwards and forwards in sympathy. As it
does so it also moves the diaphragm backwards and forwards,
generating the required soundwaves.

The three main parameters for a loudspeaker are the size of
the diaphragm, the impedance, and the power rating. In
general, the larger the loudspeaker the higher its power rating.
The power rating is normally given in watts or milliwatts
r.m.s., and it is important not to exceed it. To do so risks
having the speech coil burn out, or the unit could literally rip
itself apart. The power ratings of miniature loudspeakers are
often quite low, at around 100 milliwatts to 300 milliwatts
(0.1 watts to 0.3 watts). These components are mostly quite
tough and can withstand quite severe overloads. The only
likely ill effect is a substantial degradation of what is likely to
already be a rather mediocre audio quality.

The nearest thing to a standard loudspeaker impedance is
8 ohms, which is by far the most popular impedance. Some
high power types have an impedance of 4 ohms though, and I
have occasionally encountered 6 ohm types. Although 15
ohms used to be quite a common impedance for the larger

148

loudspeakers, this one now seems to have fallen from favour and is little used these days. Miniature loudspeakers mostly have an impedance of 8 ohms, but there are high impedance types which have an impedance of around 40 to 80 ohms, with 64 ohms currently being the most common of these higher impedances.

Using a loudspeaker having an impedance which is higher than the recommended one will not usually cause any major problems. The output power will be reduced, and this is likely to give a reduction in the maximum volume available. This will not necessarily happen though, as loudspeaker efficiencies vary over wide limits, and high impedance types usually have relatively high efficiencies. Do not use a loudspeaker having a lower impedance than the minimum recommended one for the amplifier (or whatever) in question. This could cause excessive currents to flow in the equipment driving the loudspeaker, possibly causing considerable damage to it.

The arrangement used in magnetic headphones and earpieces is basically the same as that used for loudspeakers. Headphones seem to be available in a variety of impedances these days. High impedance types having an impedance of about 1k to 4k seem to be a rarity these days. They are quite sensitive, and will produce reasonable volume levels from moderate signal voltages and quite low currents (sometimes less than a milliamp). The audio quality of many high impedance headphones is not particularly good though. They are mainly used in communications applications rather than hi-fi ones. Medium impedance types (about 25 to 600 ohms) are the most common type these days, and are mainly sold as replacements for personal stereo units. These mostly offer quite good sensitivity, together with reasonable audio quality.

Low impedance headphones vary enormously in terms of sensitivity and audio quality. They are mainly intended to be used with the headphone output of hi-fi equipment, but a few types are intended to be driven direct from the output of a power amplifier (the headphone sockets of hi-fi amplifiers are normally connected to the outputs of the amplifiers via attenuators). Last, and probably least, there are the low impedance magnetic earpieces. These are also known as "dynamic" earphones. They have an impedance of 8 ohms, together with low sensitivity as they are designed to be driven direct from the small power amplifiers found in portable radios, cassette recorders, etc. The quality of most earphones of this type seems to leave much to be desired.

Some hi-fi speakers use electro-static forces rather than magnetic ones to move the diaphragm, but this type of loud-speaker is not in general use. Hi-fi tweeters (speakers designed only to handle high frequency sounds) sometimes rely on the Piezo effect. Certain types of naturally occurring crystals and man-made ceramic materials exhibit this property. Rochelle salt is an example of a naturally occurring crystal that has this property. If a piece of a suitable substance has two electrodes fitted on opposite surfaces, placing a voltage across the electrodes will cause the assembly to twist or bend slightly. The greater the voltage, the larger the distortion. Furthermore, reversing the polarity of the signal causes it to twist or bend in the opposite direction. Physically coupling the unit to a diaphragm gives a simple but effective loudspeaker.

The same effect is used in crystal earphones. These are remarkably sensitive, and will produce an audible output from signals of just a few millivolts r.m.s., and high volume from less than one volt r.m.s. They have a fairly high input impedance, and require very little drive current. The loading characteristics of a crystal earphone are totally different to those of a magnetic type. Whereas a magnetic earphone or headphones have a fairly low d.c. resistance and are primarily inductive in nature, there is a very high resistance of many megohms through a crystal earphone. They are primarily capacitive in nature, and from the electrical point of view a crystal earphone "looks" very much like a capacitor of around 2n to 20n to the circuit that is driving it.

Piezo electric resonators are a form of loudspeaker, but they are mainly intended for use in alarm circuits. They only operate efficiently over a very limited range of frequencies, and the alarm generator circuits are designed to produce frequencies where the resonators offer peak efficiency, or something very close to it. The resonators are usually in the form of flat disks about 20 millimetres in diameter, and contained in plastic cases that aid high volume over the

150

appropriate frequency range. They are also available as uncased units, which are mainly used in applications where only low volume levels are required (audio alarms in watches, etc.). These uncased units can actually provide high efficiencies and volume levels, but only if they are mounted in a suitable enclosure. The point of these units is that they will operate with minimal input powers. The cased units when operated at suitable frequencies will produce ear-splitting volume levels from input levels of a few milliwatts. As pointed out previously, ordinary moving coil loudspeakers are not very efficient, and need power levels of a few hundred milliwatts r.m.s. or more in order to produce high volume levels.

The Piezo effect can be, and is, used in reverse. Vibrations of the crystal cause small electrical charges to be generated across the electrodes. This is the basis of crystal microphones, which are somewhat less common than they once were. This is perhaps due to their high output impedance. In fact their output impedance is largely dependent on frequency, and although it is quite low at high frequencies, it can be around one megohm at the lowest audio frequencies. A crystal microphone is effectively a voltage generator in series with a capacitor of a few nanofarads in value. It is the low value of this coupling capacitor that gives the high output impedance at low frequencies. The practical consequence of this is that a crystal microphone needs to feed into an input impedance of about 1 megohm or more in order to provide a good bass response. Such high input impedances were easily obtained in the days of valve circuits, but were less easily achieved using the early transistors. High input impedances can be achieved quite easily using modern f.e.t.s and operational amplifiers, but crystal microphones would now seem to have fallen from favour and are little used these days. The output level from a crystal microphone is quite high by microphone standards incidentally, at typically around 5 to 10 millivolts r.m.s. Long connecting cables can not be used with crystal microphones. The capacitance of the microphone plus the capacitance in the cable provide a form of potential divider action, and seriously attenuate the output signal.

The Piezo electric effect is also applied to record player pick-ups, but the output level from these crystal and ceramic pick-ups is very much higher than that from a crystal microphone. This is simply due to the fact that they receive more energy than a crystal microphone, rather than any fundamental difference in their operating method. The output level exceeds one volt r.m.s. in some cases.

A final type of Piezo electric microphone/loudspeaker is the ultrasonic transducer. The types that are generally available to amateur users are intended for operation at about 40kHz, where they offer peak performance. They are intended for remote control and burglar alarm applications, and are normally sold in pairs (one for the transmitter and one for the receiver). Sometimes the two units are identical, but in some cases there are specific types for transmission and reception. In my experience of these components there is very little difference between the transmitting and receiving transducers, and getting them the wrong way round often has no noticeable affect on the performance of the system! Although ultrasonic transducers will operate at reasonable efficiency over a wider range of frequencies than their intended very narrow band, note that they are "deaf" to all but the highest audio frequencies when used as microphones, and produce very little output at audio frequencies when used as loudspeakers. They are really only usable in ultrasonic applications.

A moving coil (or "dynamic") microphone is essentially the same as a loudspeaker in principle, but with vibrations of the diaphragm moving the voice coil and generating corresponding a.c. signals in it. The diaphragm of a loudspeaker is quite large so that it is reasonably efficient (although most loudspeakers still achieve very low levels of efficiency in absolute terms). In modern microphones the diaphragm is normally quite small in order to aid good audio quality, particularly good high frequency response. The output level from low impedance (200 ohm and 600 ohm) dynamic microphones is quite low, with about 200 microvolts being typical for the 200 ohm type. The 600 ohm units generally have slightly higher output levels, but are unlikely to exceed one millivolt r.m.s. These microphones are usually quite inexpensive, and are the type widely sold as replacements for use with cassette recorders and decks.

High impedance dynamic microphones achieve higher output voltages, and around 2 millivolts to 5 millivolts is typical for a 50k impedance type. Some high impedance types actually consist of a low impedance microphone insert plus a step-up transformer. In fact virtually all high impedance dynamic microphones seem to use this arrangement. Some of the more expensive microphones of this type have balanced output lines, and will give very low levels of "hum" pick-up in the connecting cable if they are used with a balanced input.

Electret microphones are a relatively new type, and offer excellent performance at moderate cost. They operate in a manner which is similar to crystal types, but is not strictly speaking the same. They have a very high output impedance, but are normally equipped with a simple built-in f.e.t. pre-amplifier stage. Unlike most other types of microphone, electret types therefore require a power supply, which is normally in the form of an integral 1.5 volt battery. Due to the inclusion of a preamplifier the output impedance of an electret microphone is quite low, and they are used as an alternative to low impedance dynamic microphones. Some have a built-in step-up transformer and can be used with inputs that are intended for operation with high impedance dynamic microphones

Meters
The most simple form of meter movement is the moving iron type. These are relatively little used in electronic instruments as they are difficult to produce with high sensitivities, and their scaling is non-linear. The scale is well spread out at the low end, and becomes increasingly cramped at the high end. The pointer has an iron pole piece at its bottom end, and this rests alongside an electro-magnet under quiescent conditions. Putting a current through the electro-magnet results in it repelling the pole piece, and producing a deflection of the pointer. The greater the current the larger the deflection of the pointer. Although moving iron meters are less than ideal in certain respects, they do have the advantages of being relatively cheap to produce, and they are also quite tough by meter standards (but are still quite delicate in absolute terms).

153

The meters used in electronic applications are mostly of the moving coil type. This consists basically of a coil of wire on a light aluminium former to which the pointer is fitted, and a ring shaped magnet with a small section missing. The coil, rotating around a soft iron core, is fitted in the space provided by this missing section, and it is therefore between the north and south poles of the magnet. Modern meters mostly have transparent front covers, and these enable you to see the coil and magnet, together with the (usually) jewelled movement on which the pointer/coil assembly pivots.

This gives a very simple set-up, but the way in which it functions is something less than obvious. It looks symmetrical and likely to give zero deflection of the pointer when a current is fed through the coil. In fact the magnetic field of the coil is perpendicular to that of the permanent magnet, and energising the coil with a current of the correct polarity results in the coil rotating, and giving the desired forwards deflection of the pointer. Furthermore, there is good linearity between the applied current and the deflection of the pointer. In a practical meter there is a coiled spring which brings the pointer back to zero when the coil is de-energised. There is almost invariably an adjustment screw which operates via this spring, and enables the pointer to be adjusted so that it accurately aligned with the zero marking of the scale under quiescent conditions.

Moving coil meters are high quality instruments that are much used in electronics, even in these days of digital just about everything. They offer a reasonably inexpensive and very simple means of obtaining a quite high degree of accuracy. In terms of accuracy they are probably less good than most digital readout systems, but they are perfectly adequate for most purposes. They can be made quite sensitive, and moving coil meters having full scale deflections (f.s.d.s) of just 50 microamps are readily available. The only major drawback of moving coil meters is that they are relatively delicate, especially the larger types (which are also very expensive). Dropping a moving coil meter from a few feet onto the floor could well damage the meter movement beyond repair.

Connectors

The range of connectors currently available is vast, and this is one type of component that seems to rival semiconductors in terms of the number of pages occupied in components catalogues. There is insufficient space available here to go into a detailed description of every available type. Instead, the more common types, plus some of the less common ones are listed, together with suggested uses for each one, plus any other important facts.

DIN Connectors

All DIN connectors are primarily designed for use in audio equipment. However, they are used in numerous low and medium frequency applications, including such things as computer cassette interfaces, digital serial interfaces, and video applications. There are numerous types available, but these are the ones that are readily available. The applications listed are just some typical ones, and as already pointed out, these connectors are to be found on a diverse range of equipment.

2 way	Mainly used for loudspeakers in low — medium power systems.
3 way	Mainly used for monophonic audio equipment.
5 way 180 degree	Standard stereo audio connector, and MIDI.
5 way 240 degree	Audio and monitors.
5 way "Domino"	Audio, monitors, serial interfaces.
6 way	Computer cassette interfaces.
7 way	Computer cassette interfaces.
8 way Offset	Rare.
8 way circular	Rare.

Other L.F. Connectors

Phono	A 2 way co-axial connector that is much used in audio systems in preference (or in addition to) DIN types. Also used in a variety of applications up to v.h.f. (very high frequencies).

2.5mm jack	2 way, cassette recorder remote control switch and earphones.
3.5mm jack	2 way, cassette recorder microphones, earphones, and general low frequency use.
3.5mm stereo jack	3 way, personal stereo unit headphone connector.
¼″ jack	2 way, also known as standard jack, used as general purpose audio connector, especially in communications and electronic music.
¼″ stereo jack	3 way, headphone connector for hi-fi equipment.
XLR	3 way, very high quality (and expensive) audio connector.

High Frequency Connectors

Standard co-axial	2 way, 75 ohm impedance, television aerials, and general high frequency use.
N series	2 way, 50 ohm impedance, CB radio and other communications equipment.
Car radio	2 way, only seems to be used for car radios.

Computer Connectors

9 way D type	Switch type joysticks, and monitors.
15 way D type	Potentiometer style joysticks, and general computer use.
25 way D type	Parallel and serial ports, plus general computer use.
Edge connectors	Various numbers of ways and pitches, home computer expansion ports, and general computer use.
DIN 41612	32, 64, and 96 way, computer expansion buses.
IDC	Various numbers of ways, general computer use, including internal connections to keyboards etc.
IEEE-488	36 way, IEEE-488 interfaces, a Centronics type parallel printer interfaces.

156

SCART	21 way, monitors (general VDU connector, not just computer monitors).

Power Connectors

Euro connector	3 way, mains lead to equipment.
4mm terminal post	1 way, power supply outputs.
1.3mm	2 way, external p.s.u. to "Walkman".
2.1mm	2 way, external p.s.u. to cassette recorder, etc.
2.5mm	2 way, external p.s.u. to cassette recorder, etc.

Index

159

Notes

Please note following is a list of other titles that are available in our range of Radio, Electronics and Computer books.

These should be available from all good Booksellers, Radio Component Dealers and Mail Order Companies.

However, should you experience difficulty in obtaining any title in your area, then please write directly to the Publisher enclosing payment to cover the cost of the book plus adequate postage.

If you would like a complete catalogue of our entire range of Radio, Electronics and Computer Books then please send a Stamped Addressed Envelope to:

BERNARD BABANI (publishing) LTD
THE GRAMPIANS
SHEPHERDS BUSH ROAD
LONDON W6 7NF
ENGLAND